p 12, 19, 21, 22, 27

SIGNS OF SAFETY

*A Solution and Safety Oriented
Approach to Child Protection*

SIGNS OF SAFETY

A Solution and Safety Oriented
Approach to Child Protection

Andrew Turnell
Steve Edwards

W.W. NORTON & COMPANY • New York • London

For information about permission to reproduce selections
from this book, write to
Permissions, W. W. Norton & Company, Inc., 500 Fifth Avenue
New York, NY 10110

Composition by Bytheway Publishing Services
Manufacturing by Haddon Craftsmen

Library of Congress Cataloging-in-Publication Data

Turnell, Andrew.
    Signs of safety : a solution and safety oriented approach to child
protection / Andrew Turnell, Steve Edwards.
        p.   cm.
    Includes bibliographical references and index.
    ISBN 0-393-70300-2
    1. Child welfare.   2. Child welfare—Australia.   3. Child abuse—
Investigation.   4. Social work with children.   5. Family social
work.   I. Edwards, Steve.   II. Title.
HV713.T87   1999
362.7'0994—dc21   99-25147   CIP

W. W. Norton & Company, Inc., 500 Fifth Avenue, New York, N.Y. 10110
www.wwnorton.com
W. W. Norton & Company Ltd., 10 Coptic Street, London WC1A 1PU

15 16 17 18 19 20

This book is for the children,
and we dedicate it to our children:
Jacksie and Greta, Jeremy and Keayn.

Foreword

Child Protection Services (CPS) workers are criticized either for intruding too much into the integrity and sacred privacy of a family or for not doing enough to "pull" children from abusive and neglectful adults who do not deserve to be parents. Workers have been called everything from "baby snatchers" and "soft police" to "bleeding hearts" and "baby killers." CPS has been on the receiving end of critique and scrutiny from all segments of society for some time. Practitioners writing about this difficult branch of child welfare risk becoming the target of criticism from those who think workers are "too social worky" or "naively optimistic" about the "nasty" and "evil" parents who take pleasure in abusing helpless and vulnerable children. I applaud Andrew Turnell and Steven Edwards for their courage in staking a position in a field that can be very confusing to workers who are liable to make mistakes, yet asked to "solve social problems one case at a time" (Thorpe, 1994).

The field of child welfare has a tumultuous history of searching for definitive solutions. Being rediscovered by physicians, who identified "battered child syndrome" (Kempe et al., 1962), was both a blessing and a problem, as was the necessity for legal mandate. Medical and legal imperatives, coupled with public outrage and societal wishes to protect helpless children, evolved into the confusing, often contradictory practice that is modern child protection. The maltreatment of children is a complex and complicated issue that does not lend itself to simple explanations or solutions. Similarly, writing about this difficult and convoluted issue is not an easy task. Yet the authors have done a credible job of distilling practical concepts and techniques that workers in the trenches will find very useful.

The field of child welfare is currently undergoing a paradigm shift. Social workers have been challenged by innovative thinkers and advocates who insist that they adopt a "strength perspective" (Saleeby, 1992) rather than a deficit point of view toward clients. The traditional social service philosophy, in which service recipients were seen as deficient in their ability to make decisions for themselves or unable to act in their own best interest, is being questioned. The trend in mental health and human services is to view CPS clients as more than bundles of problems, depositories of personal failure, and victims of abuse. Unlike the "scientific" or "medical" approach, which is generated from a problem-solving model, the new perspective insists that solution-building (DeJong & Berg, 1998) involves turning away from a focus on deficits and concentrating on the discovery of resources, however small (de Shazer, 1991), to expose building blocks for change. In addition, the very concept of the "helping" relationship is changing from the traditional approach, wherein the expert has all the answers, to an approach where collaboration with the client, even an abusive and neglectful parent, is both possible and recommended.

The practice that results from this type of thinking is creating an uncomfortable challenge to the typical picture of CPS, in which the worker is viewed as a hero, rushing in to rescue the helpless child from the clutches of a parental monster who inflicts only pain and suffering. Increasingly, child protection workers are realizing that the most empowering and caring activity we can engage in is to ask questions of those we serve. A recently published book, *Rose's Story* (1991), is a stark account of how one well-meaning child welfare worker after another failed to ask questions of a child they were trying to serve. This is a powerful reminder that we are most caring, loving, and respectful of clients when we ask questions and listen to their ideas on how to improve their own lives, allowing them to decide what is best for them. This book teaches us how important it is to listen to a little child, even one who appears to be confused and not very well informed.

A book by Anne Fadiman, *The Spirit Catches You and You Fall Down* (1997), illustrates the disastrous consequences when well-meaning, thoughtful, intelligent medical experts who want to "do the right thing" come up against Hmong refugee parents who want to cherish and care for their child in a way that makes sense to them. In such cases, it is easy to blame failure on language barriers and cultural differences, but we know that we can use hands and gestures, tone of voice, and inflections to convey meaning. We can listen.

Today, child protection workers are challenged to reconcile the seemingly mutually exclusive goals of ensuring the child's safety and maintaining the parent's dignity. We must also learn to separate the phenomena of economic disadvantage and poverty from neglect. Increasing understanding of diversity and the complexity of our world requires us to reexamine all the traditionally held ideas of how to ensure safety and protect children. As we reconceptualize the *helping* relationship as a *collaborative* relationship, *Signs of Safety* will be a valuable resource.

I have long advocated for changing the name of Child Protective Services (CPS) to Family Protective Services (FPS). When we set out to "protect" a child, we presuppose that the thing we are protecting the child from is his or her parents. The concept of child protection automatically pits the child against the parent, since a child cannot exist without a parent, and one ceases to be a parent without a child. This thinking leads to the adversarial practice that has dominated the field, but we are finally coming to recognize that "blood is thicker than social service (or child protection service)."

Turnell and Edwards explain how to ask questions that are useful in creating safety for the child and expressing respect for the parent. In doing so, the authors challenge the traditional, paternalistic view that professionals always know what's best for their clients. In addition, they offer numerous case examples from the front line that allow good insight into how to think about, plan, and organize the development of a relationship with clients who are rightfully reluctant to trust anyone from the official sector. In the process, they offer tools not only for workers, but for parents as well, so they can assess their own situation, motivation, and progress, and determine possible steps to achieve their goals. The authors' high regard for clients' wishes and desires is shown by their insistence on listening to these client goals. This is the centerpiece of their work.

Signs of Safety represents not only a gentle and loving approach to protection work, but also a hopeful and respectful way to build solutions and ensure safety for the entire family. I highly recommend this book to those who are determined to "make a difference" in someone's life.

Insoo Kim Berg
Co-author, *Building Solutions in Child Protective Services*
Milwaukee, Wisconsin

Contents

SIGNS OF SAFETY

A Solution and Safety Oriented
Approach to Child Protection

Beginning with a Question:
An Introduction

A GLOBAL ISSUE

Child protection professionals are involved with vulnerable, at-risk children, some of whom will be or have been hurt and a few who will inevitably die. The work is carried out in an environment where the community, media, politicians, and others are quick to criticize any perceived errors in judgment or practice. Child protection workers are frequently damned when they do intervene and damned when they don't. In this context, the first impulse of most professionals is to take as much control as possible in the potentially volatile situations they face. However, in taking control, do the professionals, whether they be social workers, police, doctors, or judges, know the totality of what's wrong in each case? Do they have all the answers to the problem? Isn't it important to relinquish some of this control by listening carefully to the family and parents involved? Can we aspire to build a working relationship with parents, thereby creating increased safety for the child(ren)?

If child protection professionals carry out their work with little or no reference to the views and needs of the families and parents involved, then a fundamental premise of this book is undone, and, probably, the material herein will make little sense. If, however, partnership with the family is something that is worth aspiring to in child protection practice, then this book may well be useful.

Whether the relevant professionals should take on the role of the expert with all the answers or adopt a stance of fostering collaboration with families is, in fact, the subject of lively debate in child

1

protection circles around the world. We stand squarely behind the belief in partnership as central to good child protection practice. However, while partnership is inherently appealing (almost like "mom and apple pie," as Americans might say), in the charged environment of child protection, where children are at risk, we must leap many hurdles and break out of traditional constraints if the ideal is to be realized.

In creating the signs of safety approach to child protection casework, we have been attempting to find an answer to the question: *How can child protection professionals actually build partnerships with parents where there is suspected or substantiated child abuse or neglect?* In introducing this book, we want to describe our own struggle with this question. It is an important story to tell, since it is not only the history of the development of the signs of safety, but also a story that provides the human context in which to locate the professional work we have undertaken.

The Local Question: How Could This Apply to a Child Protection Investigation?

The summer of 1988/89 in Perth, Western Australia, saw the beginning of a new service for families with rebellious or distressed teenagers. Centrecare Marriage and Family Service (a Catholic counseling and welfare organization) had won a contract from the state government's statutory child welfare agency to provide therapy to parents and teenagers in conflict. The funding and contract for the new service provided for two full-time positions for counselors to see 250 families each year. Faced with the imperatives of that equation, the new workers immediately settled on brief therapy as the mode of intervention for their new service, Parent-Teen Link.

In Perth, the most isolated city in the most isolated country on the planet, it is perfectly possible that, a mere six months after a group begins an undertaking in almost any field, they find themselves being regarded as the city's experts in that endeavor. So it was for the three part-time workers who filled the two full-time positions. No sooner had they started the service than they were being asked to tell other professionals what they were doing and to provide training in brief therapy. At this stage, the child protection workers referring the teenagers and their parents were the ones asking for training. Inevitably, the presentations, training, and discussions with the child protection workers led them to ask: Okay, this brief therapy stuff looks useful and seems to work, but how does it apply to a child protection investigation and the subsequent casework? Since those very early days (when one of us was working for the statutory child welfare agency and the other in the Parent-Teen Link program), we have been attempting to answer that question.

At the heart of all brief therapy approaches is the notion that the best way the helping professional can facilitate change is by building a cooperative relationship with the client (see Fisch, Weakland, & Segal, 1982, and de Shazer, 1984). Therefore, questioning the application of brief therapy to child protection is fundamentally another way of asking: Is it possible to develop a cooperative relationship with clients in the emotionally charged environment of child protection investigation and casework where children are at risk?

In early 1991, Steve de Shazer and Insoo Kim Berg, founders of solution-focused brief therapy, came to Perth as guests of the workers in Parent-Teen Link. Insoo, it turned out, was also exploring the same question and, at the end of three days' work, related the following story to a small group that included one of the authors (Andrew Turnell). Insoo had participated in a series of child protection interviews, one of which involved talking to a father who had physically abused his daughter for several years. At one point in the interview Insoo asked the perpetrator, "Have there been any times when you have been in a rage but resisted the urge to hit your daughter?" This story demonstrated the use of a typical solution-focused brief therapy inquiry (an exception question) in a child protection scenario and served to quicken our interest in pursuing the application of brief therapy to child protection.

Following the visit of de Shazer and Berg, and inspired by them, the other author (Steve Edwards, at that time drawing on 14 years' experience in the statutory child welfare agency in Western Australia) began to actively experiment with various solution-focused therapy techniques in child protection investigations and casework. On one such occasion Steve was interviewing a girl and felt little progress was being made. Changing tack, he asked a typical solution-focused brief therapy question: "Let's imagine that tonight you go to bed, and, while you're sleeping, a miracle happens. The result of this miracle is that you wake up tomorrow morning and all the problems we're talking about are solved. How would you know? What would be happening differently?" This question is a variation of what is commonly known as a miracle question (de Shazer, 1988). The girl's answer was striking. She stated "Dad would be dead!" Although the girl said little else, the question had broken the impasse and generated useful information. Steve offered the girl the opportunity to talk with a female child protection officer, to whom she disclosed, not surprisingly, that she was being sexually abused by her father.

On another investigation regarding allegations of neglect, Steve felt that something different was definitely called for. The mother involved had been investigated on two previous occasions over the previous three years. Her only child had been removed from the home on several occasions, and the woman had an extensive psychiatric history. Taking the view that the problem had been well and truly covered on previous occasions, Steve initiated a dialogue centered around the woman's ideas about solving the problem. While the discussion generated specific plans, which the client was willing to attempt, the highly experienced social worker who accompanied Steve on this home visit was skeptical. He could see that the woman was engaged and would perhaps do what she had talked about, but he was not sure that the allegation of neglect had been properly addressed.

As is perhaps always the case in the early development of innovative practice, for every possible answer that is considered, many more questions are generated. To look more closely at the application of brief therapy to child protection casework, Steve decided to undertake a social work honors project and dissertation (Edwards, 1991) examining the utility of solution-focused brief therapy in the case of one family who had a long history of involvement in the child welfare process.

At about this time, both authors began to regularly collaborate in the clinical setting when Steve joined the Parent-Teen Link team one night per week to observe and then facilitate therapy with the families of teenagers. Before and after the clinical work, discussions would often turn to Steve's latest attempts to apply brief therapy ideas to his daytime work.

Local Development

By this more or less informal process, our ideas were beginning to take shape. In 1993 Steve joined the Parent-Teen Link team on a one-year temporary assignment from the statutory child protection agency*. This provided the opportunity to explore our questions

---

*Usually referred to throughout this book as either "the statutory agency" or simply "the agency."

more systematically, particularly when Dr. Larry Hopwood (then the training director of the Brief Family Therapy Center in Milwaukee) joined the authors and their colleagues in Perth for a one-month period in November 1993. He led our team through a strategic planning process that enabled us to describe the necessary steps involved in a more systematic exploration of the application of brief therapy to child protection. This planning process marked the conception of the signs of safety approach.

To test our ideas, it was evident that we needed to collaborate with a group of practicing child protection workers. To this end we contacted John Hancock, manager of a large rural district* of the Western Australian statutory child welfare agency, asking if there might be a handful of workers interested in working with us on a number of cases to explore our ideas. John immediately suggested that all child protection workers in his region participate in a project involving all child protection cases work for a six-month period. We were both excited and daunted by the prospect of "jumping in the deep end" so quickly, but when life offers a challenge/opportunity like this, the only real option is to take it.

The three months between December 1993 and February 1994 saw preparations begin in earnest. Two advance meetings were held: first between ourselves and the region's casework supervisors and managers, and then a second with all field staff. The purpose of both meetings was to establish the goals of the project for management, field staff, and ourselves as consultants (Edwards & Turnell, 1995, fully describes the process and goals).

Management was looking for an approach that would increase the confidence of child protection workers in their own practice and enable them more readily to make and commit to assessments/judgments based on a balance of information regarding danger and safety. It was hoped that the six-month project would also enhance collaboration and teamwork in the agency. The workers' aspirations were similar in intent, with a greater emphasis on building skills. They were looking for an approach that would help them get unstuck in difficult and protracted cases, that was flexible and responsive to diverse client situations and cultures, that was applicable from intake through to case closure, and that would enable them to draw on client's strengths while being mindful of the safety of the child(ren)

---

*Australians would use the term "country region."

involved. Our own goals essentially involved exploring our question further by developing a specific safety and solution-oriented approach that could be field-tested by the workers. If we were successful, we would see the child protection workers engaging with and actually using the approach.

In this same preparatory period we undertook a literature review of consumer research within the child protection field. This initial search, identified as a step in the strategic planning process, was to evolve into a major theme in the signs of safety approach. In our view, the messages from consumers about their experiences of being subjected to child protection intervention are vital information for developing good practice. We also prepared a workbook that described the approach, offered an extensive list of safety factors (matched to the schema for considering child protection risk factors used in Western Australia), included flow charts for implementation, and presented the first signs of safety assessment forms. Joe Goerke, a social worker with 20 years child protection experience, provided continuous feedback on our ideas and writing (as he has done ever since). In early March 1994, the project commenced when we provided two days' training in solution-focused brief therapy and the newly named signs of safety approach to child protection for all the staff (field staff through to managers) who were to be involved in the six-month project.

Anyone who knows anything about child protection knows we had set ourselves an impossible task. To say the least, it was unrealistic to expect child protection workers to take a newly articulated approach, described to them (as best we could, but nowhere near well enough) in two days, and to implement the approach in every child protection case from day one of the six-month project. While the workers *were* interested, it took three months before they really began to engage with the approach systematically. Typical of any child welfare agency, workers had a wide range of professional orientations and experience, from new graduates to workers with many years of hard-won experience. We were to learn time and again that the best way to enable workers to use this approach was through the case examples of fellow workers. Two examples that were to provide such a catalyst were presented during the third of the project's monthly half-day consultations.

Diane Fuller and Kerry Bein were required to investigate a case of possible sexual abuse. The alleged perpetrator had been charged with sexual abuse offenses (for which he was subsequently jailed) relating to a young girl who was the daughter of a previous partner. The man was now in a new relationship, living on an isolated farm with a new partner who had a daughter of similar age. Further details of this case are provided elsewhere (Turnell & Edwards, 1997). It is enough to say here that, following three interviews and a thorough consideration of indicators of possible harm *and* signs of safety, a report was prepared and authorized by management that recommended the child remain in the home. In a second case, Heath Ridley utilized one practice element of the approach (exception questioning) while taking an intake phone call. The information generated by this questioning removed the need for an investigation that would likely have been very difficult and involved the potential for violence toward the worker.

Motivated by their colleagues' case examples, the other child protection workers began to make use of the approach. We cannot claim that all workers used the approach in every case. However, the new approach certainly did have a constructive impact on child protection practice in the region (Edwards & Turnell, 1995, describes the workers' feedback). From this first project, we learned an extraordinary amount about the direct application of our ideas to child protection casework, and, just as importantly, we also learned invaluable lessons about how to facilitate use of the approach by the organization and its professionals.

Since that first project, through a process of ongoing collaboration and subsequent six-month projects with child protection workers in Perth and rural districts of Western Australia, the signs of safety approach has been increasingly refined and developed. The initial workbook was rewritten and the training process both extended and refined. We learned time and again that the approach was most quickly assimilated when we:

- Assumed and elicited the considerable experience and good practice of child protection workers we were training.
- Based our training on actual case material.
- Collaborated with workers over an extended period, fostering and also learning from their experience in using the signs of safety model.

As with the first project, our touchstone for success has always been whether what we are saying makes sense to child protection practitioners and whether it is used by them in their casework.

Therefore, we have included many case examples throughout this book of how child protection workers in the field have made use of the signs of safety model in their casework.

International Contributions

The development of the signs of safety approach has been accelerated and enhanced by our connections with practitioners, researchers, and child protection agencies in other states of Australia and around the world. As mentioned earlier, many in the child protection field believe that professionals should retain all the power and authority in the delivery of services. However, through international contacts we have become aware of many agencies and professionals who, like us, perceive partnership with clients as both viable and beneficial. Efforts in the direction of collaborative practice in child protection have given birth to different programs in different places throughout the world. Below we describe the work of those who have directly influenced and contributed to the development of the signs of safety approach.

Research with child protection service recipients is the context for our exploration of partnership, since families who have been subject to child protection investigations consistently describe their wish for increased collaboration between themselves and statutory workers. We have been directly influenced in our work by collaborating with Laurie MacKinnon, Sharon McCallum, and Elaine Farmer, who have undertaken major studies of service recipients in Australia, Canada, and the United Kingdom respectively. Both MacKinnon and McCallum have designed collaborative practice approaches to casework as a result of their research: MacKinnon (1998) describes a treatment approach, while McCallum (1992, 1995) offers participatory models for statutory work.

For the past four years we have been in close contact with the "resolutions" team of Susie Essex, John Gumbleton, and Colin Luger at the National Society for the Prevention of Cruelty to Children, Bristol, in the UK. This team has designed a remarkable treatment approach, responding to the child protection issues of families where there has been substantiated physical or sexual abuse and where parents are denying responsibility—the so-called "untreatable" families (Essex, Gumbleton, & Luger, 1996). Between them they draw on more than 30 years of child protection investigative experience. In addition, they collaborate closely with many of the researchers and academics who are sustaining an ongoing analysis of child protection practice in the UK. From this broad base of experience, the team offers invaluable commentary on our work and continues to demonstrate to us that a safety-building/safety-focused approach can be successful with the hardest child protection cases.

Although our work approaches child protection risk assessment from the perspective of existing and potential safety, interactions with professionals grounded in traditional risk assessment designed to assess harm and danger have been crucial in its evolution. We have collaborated with Julie Boffa, from the Department of Human Services in Victoria, Australia, and Craig Smith, from the New Zealand Child and Young Persons Services, who are both involved in developing and implementing risk assessment frameworks. Discussions with these colleagues have facilitated our integration of the assessment of the issues of safety and danger.

Recently we have had the chance to collaborate with Ted Keys, a family-based programs coordinator at the State Office for Services to Children and Families in Oregon. Ted is one of the creators of the family unity meeting conferencing model. Comparing with him experiences both practical and philosophical regarding the development and implementation of a partnership-based child protection approach has deepened and strengthened our perspective.

We also keep in close contact with our mentor, Insoo Kim Berg, who is currently involved in implementing a solution-building approach to child protection practice across all levels (field staff through to senior management) of the statutory child welfare agency in the state of Michigan.

Throughout the world there is a clear call from researchers, academics, and policymakers for increased partnership in child protection practice. The structured implementation of this idea has been explored primarily in "down stream" child protection activities, namely case conferencing and treatment. As far as we know, the signs of safety approach is one of the first to pursue partnership at the "front end" of the child protection process, namely intake, investigation, and assessment, and then to follow this logic through to case closure.

THIS BOOK

From its base in Western Australia, the signs of safety approach has spread to various places around the world. This book sets out to describe the thinking that informs the approach, the application

of the model from the initial intake procedures to case closure, and
ideas from our experience regarding training in the approach and
its implementation in child protection organizations.

- Chapters 1 and 2 provide an introduction to the conceptual and
  theoretical framework that underpins the signs of safety approach.
- Chapter 3 provides an overall introduction to the practice elements of the model.
- Chapters 4 through 8 overtly explore how the approach can be
  implemented at the stages of intake, investigation, assessment,
  case planning, ongoing casework, and case closure.
- Chapter 9 attends to the broader considerations of training in the
  approach, with particular emphasis on supervising and amplifying
  good practice.

Since this is a practice-oriented book, we offer many case examples
featuring child protection workers who have been continually using
this approach. To meet the needs of workers in the field for practical
guidance, chapters 4 through 7 follow the application of the signs
of safety approach to a single case from intake through investigation,
assessment, and planning stages.

Our primary purpose is to give child protection workers the ideas
and skills to begin to implement this approach during contacts with
clients, mindful that, if it is to be well implemented, a parallel
organizational response is needed. We will have been successful in
our endeavor if, upon reading this book, readers feel sufficiently
inspired and equipped to try some of our ideas.

CHAPTER ONE

Child Protection: A Global Perspective

SEEKING ANSWERS TO STRAIGHTFORWARD QUESTIONS

The taxi driver was a pretty laid-back and laconic character who talked to us sagely about politics and football. However, when we answered his question about what we did for a living—telling him that we worked in child protection—he became more animated. Our cabby immediately peppered us with questions: "How could anyone do that to their own kids?" "Is there really more of it goin' on, like the papers say, or do we just talk about it more now?" "There's nothin' you can do for people like that—you just have to lock 'em up, don't you?"

While the taxi driver's questions were constructed in layman's terms, his strong reaction and even the actual questions mirror the intense engagement of child protection professionals with their work over the past 35 years and the key issues the field has struggled with during that time. Since the modern "rediscovery" of child abuse by Kempe and his colleagues in the U.S. (Kempe, Silverman, Steele, Droegemuller, & Silver, 1962), governments, professionals, the media, and the general public have been seeking to understand what child abuse is, how often it occurs, what causes it, and what can be done to address the problem. Given that the focus of the endeavor is vulnerable children, positions and ideas are almost always passionately expressed.

One of the authors (S.E.) remembers witnessing, as a not-so-young anthropology undergraduate, the West Australian community's initial disbelief and alarm, generated by the First Australian National Conference on the Battered Child held in Perth during August 1975. (At this time Australia was about 10 years behind the U.S. in its focus on child maltreatment.) However, as in other countries, this initial shock very soon evolved into determination to address the problem, since at that time there was considerable confidence that appropriate professional responses would go a long way to eradicating it. Kempe and Kempe (1978), for example, believed that abusive parents could be identified with 76% accuracy within 24 hours of childbirth. Unfortunately, the clear-eyed, energetic, confident child protection professionals of the 1960s and 70s have evolved into the overloaded, often defensive, frequently jaded, and bureaucratically dominated workers of the late 1990s.

In the U.S., which has so often led the way in the development of ideas about the causes and treatment of child maltreatment, the 1991 National Commission on Children (cited in Thompson, 1995) concluded that:

> if the nation had deliberately designed a system that would frustrate the professionals who staff it, anger the public who finance it, and abandon the children who depend on it, it could not have not done a better job than the present child welfare system. (p. 5)

Twenty to 30 years ago child protection professionals would have predicted that by the turn of the twenty-first century, they would be increasingly confident and certain about their answers to the taxi driver's questions. In reality, however, the answers to those questions are probably more elusive now than ever before (which is one of the reasons most professionals involved in child protection would rather not admit to the work they do at parties or in places like taxis).

Describing and Quantifying
the Problem

One thing that cannot be questioned, however, is that child protection professionals the world over are facing dramatically increasing workloads. Statistics in Australia for the period 1990 to 1995 reveal that there has been an overall increase of 75% in the number of reported cases of child maltreatment, a huge increase by anyone's standard (Tomison, 1995). In the U.S., the Department of Health and Human Services estimated that in 1996, 3,006,752 children were reported to child protective services (USDHHS, 1997), a 40% increase on the 1987 figures.

Figures such as these would seem to suggest that the actual incidence of child maltreatment is increasing in developed countries around the world. However, the extent to which the increase in workloads can be equated with an increased incidence of actual child maltreatment is the subject of sometimes vehement debate. For example, Besarov (1985, 1990) and Finkelhor (1990), well-known leaders of the child protection field, have publicly aired their differences on this matter in the context of a wider but related debate.

It is undoubtedly the case that part of the escalation in workloads is due to the increased attention given to child maltreatment as countries around the globe have become more aware of child abuse and neglect at all levels of society. For example, what started in the 60s as a focus on babies who were physically abused has expanded to include maltreatment broadly defined into four categories—physical, sexual, and emotional abuse, and neglect—across children of all ages. During the past decade, sexual abuse of children seems to have been on everyone's mind—from Oprah Winfrey to church leaders facing scandals within their institutions, not to mention professionals attending the many professional conferences addressing the subject. Over the past 20 years, steadily increasing attention and, in some places, increasing notification rates have focused awareness on the issue of emotional abuse, although this aspect of child abuse has been notoriously difficult to define (Doyle, 1997). At almost any time during the past 30 years, child protection workers would tell you that neglect cases make up a large proportion of their caseload; yet this aspect of child maltreatment has never ridden a wave of popular or professional attention, since these cases are difficult not only to substantiate, but also to respond to and manage.

The four major groupings of child maltreatment have frequently been broken down into smaller differentiations and areas of concern (for example, child victims of ritual abuse, babies of drug-addicted mothers, etc.). Finklehor (in Briere, 1992) suggests that in the field there are "lumpers" and there are "splitters." By this he means that some professionals (the splitters) see the various types of maltreatment as separate areas of concern, requiring separate specialized responses. Others see the commonalities of the child maltreatment problems and seek to create a more unified child protection field. The tendency to split the services and theory of the child protection field generates ideas and models that fill journals and bookshelves, but the subsequent fragmentation between professionals and their services can result in families and children falling between the gaps.

The four major categories of child maltreatment are more or less universal in legislation around the world. At first blush, and certainly in the early writings and thinking of the field, it seemed that what constituted child abuse or neglect was self-evident and readily understood. Unfortunately, this proved not to be the case. Giovannoni and Becerra, in their seminal 1979 study, highlighted a significant lack of professional consensus. They showed that different professionals faced with the same child maltreatment scenarios applied significantly different standards regarding what constituted neglect or abuse. A similar, more recent study by Birchall and Hallett (1995) found results that, while not identical, confirmed that establishing commonly agreed-upon definitions has turned out to be no easy task in the field as a whole. This wider difficulty can and does manifest itself at the local level. It is not uncommon in our experience for tensions or even factions to arise within or between child welfare agencies regarding what should or should not be defined as abuse or neglect.

The Causes: An Increasingly Complex Picture

The U.S. has led the way in trying to answer the taxi driver's first question: Why would anyone abuse their own children? Early models, such as those propounded by Kempe and his colleagues (1962), were principally medically oriented, locating the cause of the problem in some form of parental psychopathology. Over time, these one-dimensional theories have evolved into more complex models that integrate multiple influences into an overall picture that has been likened to a jigsaw puzzle (Giardino, Christian, & Giardino, 1997). These ecological approaches to child abuse see maltreatment as arising out of an interplay of individual, family, community, societal, and cultural factors. This broader orientation began with the likes of Gil (1970) and Garbarino (1977). Since the 1960s professional attention has been directed at increasing understanding at all these different levels, and, as with the types of abuse, different aspects have been fashionable at different times. For example, at the individual and family level there has been considerable attention to "cycles of abuse" and the fact that, if a person has been abused, there is a greater likelihood he or she will abuse or be a parent of children who are abused (Buchanan, 1996). At the other end of the continuum, numerous authors have pointed out the correlation between poverty and child abuse (e.g., Gil, 1970; Pelton, 1978; Thorpe, 1994).

Other influential thinkers, such as Nigel Parton (e.g., 1985, 1996) have added further complexity by arguing that the problem of child abuse, rather than being an objective reality, is a phenomenon that is constructed in the interaction between professionals who are heavily influenced by their beliefs and knowledges, on the one hand, and the family under investigation, on the other. Thus Parton, Thorpe, and Wattam write:

> What is considered child abuse for the purpose of child protection policy and practice is much better characterized as a product of social negotiation between different values and beliefs, different social norms and professional knowledge and perspectives about children, child development and parenting. Far from being a medico-scientific reality, it is a phenomenon where moral reasoning and moral judgment are central. (1997, p. 67)

This perspective leads us to recall that much of what we consider to be child maltreatment at the end of the twentieth century might have been frowned on if known about by others one hundred years ago, but certainly would not, at that earlier time, have resulted in investigation and action by authorities.

Responding to the Problem: More Complexity

Child protection attempts to address the problem are as complex as the efforts at definition. Responses, of course, have to operate at many levels, including identification, investigation, treatment, and alternative care, to name but four. Since the causes of child maltreatment are so often framed from the perspective of the medical model, from the time of Kempe onward it has been most common to respond by providing specialized treatment for the mother, the abusive parent, and/or the family to deal with the psychological or family dysfunction that is seen to be the cause of the problem. There are many books and papers written on such treatment specializations, with America leading the way in developing a wide variety of treatment responses.

In many ways, the British response has been more "managerial," with a focus on setting up an administrative system for detecting, investigating, and processing cases (Corby, 1987). Interagency coordination of services has received considerable attention (e.g., Hallett, 1995; Hallett & Birchall, 1992). The U.S.—being such a diverse country, with what Thompson (1995, p. 6) calls "a fragmented compilation of diverse agencies"—can probably only dream of the level of service integration that has been developed in the United Kingdom, which likely leads the English-speaking world in this aspect of child protection service delivery.

While the medical model has been the dominant paradigm in child protection, there has been a shift from seeing the problem in purely medical or psychological terms toward a more socio-legal perspective. With this shift has come increased emphasis on investigative and "forensic" procedures, with particular focus on risk assessment protocols (a boom area in child protection during the 1990s). Parton (1996) argues that this orientation effectively becomes a blaming system, with its primary purpose to establish who is accountable for any given incident.

There has always been a tension in the child protection field about how to respond to very serious maltreatment. Some (for example, Dale, Davies, Morrison, & Waters, 1986; Gelles, in press; Kempe & Kempe, 1978) have argued forcefully that some families are "incurable," "dangerous," or "untreatable" and that the only valid form of intervention is permanent removal of the child(ren). It is an undeniable child protection reality that permanent removal of a child will be necessary in some families exhibiting minimal prior and future capacity to build safety for the child(ren). In tandem with these risks, the professionals involved are inevitably unable to establish a working partnership with the parents. However, the difficulty in recognizing this reality is that it immediately generates the risk of inflating the numbers of families that are seen to be untreatable. Others have wanted to discount this possibility, aware that to deem a family untreatable can amount to extinguishing its existence. It is one of the greatest conundrums of child protection: how to recognize the occasional families that cannot be assisted or coerced to provide increased safety, without demonizing excessive numbers of other families with the same, though inappropriate, label.

Whether as a permanent or temporary arrangement, alternative care has always been part of the response to the needs of maltreated children. There are many challenges to be faced in placing children away from their home, perhaps the greatest being that it is often easier to remove children than to know when to return them. Case-workers may want to believe that the child they have removed from a dangerous home is now safe. However, abuse of children in institutions and foster placements by people meant to be caring for them has been a scandal all around the world in the past decade. By and large, there has been a move toward trying to keep children in the home. Part of the momentum in this direction has evolved through the family preservation movement. The U.S. is currently in the middle of a debate that is reversing this momentum (Gelles, in press), though Pelton (1997) contends that family preservation was always more myth than reality.

However, while family preservation originated in America, adoption is still a major element of the response to child maltreatment there. Australia, in contrast, by and large jettisoned adoption as an option by the mid-1980s, with growing awareness of the long-term problems of permanently separating parents and their children. These problems have been particularly well-articulated in traumatic stories of indigenous Australians, the so-called "stolen generation." Presently, only a handful of children are adopted each year in Australia.

Influential thinkers such as Pelton in the U.S. and Parton in Britain have consistently argued that responding to child maltreatment issues by focusing primarily on child protection casework (even in aggregate) is a form of reductionism that avoids looking at the more difficult and important social, cultural, and ideological issues. In this context, Gil wrote, "There is no way of escaping the conclusion that the complete elimination of child abuse on all levels of manifestation requires a radical transformation of the prevailing unjust, inegalitarian, irrational, competitive, alienating and hierarchical social order into a just, egalitarian, rational, cooperative, humane and truly democratic decentralized one" (1970, p. 355). We have considerable sympathy for this view, but also recognize the reality that child protection workers will have to deal with many, many cases before such social change comes about.

We have provided a brief overview of professional thinking about child maltreatment, its incidence, its causes, and what to do about it, highlighting the increasing complexity of the answers. When workers get involved with a family suspected of child abuse or neglect, they know that they will probably face a difficult situation. In an ideal world, a worker would go into this encounter backed by a child protection system that functions well, a society that understands and supports the worker's role, and a body of theoretical knowledge and skills base about which there is broad professional consensus. Unfortunately, this is not the case. At every level of the child protection endeavor, increasing difficulty and complexity seem to be the principal certainty. This is surely one of the reasons why worker turnover in the field is so high.

PARTNERSHIP OR PATERNALISM?

When we began this work, one of us (S.E.) had been involved in the direct delivery of child welfare services for over 16 years. Throughout his experience in a statutory child protection agency, Steve faced the sorts of issues and complexity we have just described on a daily basis. However, he felt that much of the child protection thinking was not really helping him do his job. Steve's contention that there must be a better way of doing things was the impetus for our joint collaboration.

Thomas (1995), in a strong critique, argues that there is a trench or fault line that runs down the center of the child protection field, with thinkers, academics, and bureaucrats standing on one side and workers on the other. Theory and practice are divorced from one another and, in Thomas's view, service recipients are often to be found at the bottom of the trench. We, like Thomas, are advocates for knowledge and expertise that enable collaboration between theoreticians and practitioners and between practitioners and service recipients.

Along with Steve's direct experience of the gap between child protection theory and practice, the other foundational influence in our development of the signs of safety approach was, and is, the tradition of brief therapy (de Shazer, 1985, 1988, 1991; de Shazer et al., 1986; Watzlawick, Weakland, & Fisch, 1974; Weakland, Fisch, Watzlawick, & Bodin, 1974). One of the fundamental tenets of brief therapy is: "When what you are doing is not working, don't do more of the same, do something different." In our view, the child protection field continually engages in something that is not working. It repeatedly acts out the logic of paternalism (Calder, 1995), with professionals taking upon themselves sole responsibility for analyzing the problem of child mistreatment and generating solutions. Families are left out of this process, except to be thought of as the appropriate recipients of services at the end of this equation.

In many settings it makes perfect sense that professionals develop their specialization to such a refined and advanced level of abstraction that it is next to impossible for anyone else to understand what they are doing or thinking. In a field such as physics, for example, this is not a problem, since by and large the general public isn't that interested in learning about the properties of various sub-atomic particles or building accelerators to differentiate one from the other. However, the general public has a vital and immediate interest in a profession that might just turn up on the doorstep one day and start asking questions about how children in the household are being parented. In this context, high-powered professional expertise and knowledge frequently serve to alienate the professional from the families and vice versa. In this regard, paternalism does not serve the child protection field well, since it escalates the pressures on the professionals to get it right and widens the trench between service recipients and professionals.

In our view "doing something different" in the child protection field involves backfilling the trench between thinkers and practitioners and the divide between professionals and service recipients. Thomas has a similar vision for what he calls "the prospects for renewal" in child welfare theory and practice. He proposes that part of the solution lies in professionals who will:

> undertake the difficult task of working toward the development of a common language. What do the problem, syndrome and case status terms we use really mean? If we were to attempt to assign each an independent definition, how many would be found to be duplicative or trivial in meaning? How many are expressed in language that the public and clients can understand? What can we learn from listening to clients and the public about how they define troubling children and family behaviors? (1995, p. 244)

In critiquing the seemingly endless escalation of the role of the "professional as expert" within the child protection field, we want to emphasize that we are not opposed to professional knowledge and expertise per se. We are well aware of professional thinking and practice from different countries that have made significant contributions to collaboration between theoreticians and practitioners and between practitioners and service recipients; some of these we will describe shortly. In fact, one of the primary purposes of the signs of safety model is to offer a structure or framework that facilitates the integration of family and professional knowledge from intake through to case closure.

Focusing specifically on the casework relationship between the worker and family, John Weakland (an original founder of the brief therapy tradition) and colleague Lynn Jordan say of their experience collaborating with child protection workers in Marin County, California:

> The only avenue toward lasting protection of children—except the extreme measure of permanently removing them from the home— depends on establishing a cooperative relationship between the parent(s) and case worker. (1990, p. 53)

This quote leads us in the direction of "doing something different that can make a difference" in child protection. Quite simply, rather than proposing that professionals act as if they have primary or even sole responsibility to analyze and solve the problems, Weakland and Jordan highlight the crucial role of building partnerships with the service recipients with whom they deal, and thereby sharing the responsibility to resolve the situation. This requires professionals to think differently about how they work, step outside of the expert role, and approach the client with a genuine sense of respect and engagement.

While we have contrasted the ideas of partnership and paternalism, we actually see them as two ends of a continuum, rather than disjunctive notions. We agree with Calder (1995) that the professional must balance the two aspects of paternalism and partnership. For example, a worker at the beginning of an investigation may need to be coercive in getting parents to participate in a meeting that they don't necessarily want. However, through a careful and skillful process, the worker may well shift the relationship significantly toward cooperation and partnership by the end of that first interview. Calder states "partnership should embrace the dilution of the professional power" (p. 753); however, child protection workers cannot abandon their legal authority, so the challenge is to exercise this authority in a manner that fosters cooperation between the professional and the family.

Partnership, however, can readily be the quintessential child protection motherhood issue: almost impossible to disagree with, but nobody quite knows what it is. Although the concept remains somewhat elusive, we have defined partnership in the following terms:

partnership exists when both the statutory agency and the family cooperate and make efforts to achieve specific, mutually understood goals. Partnership cannot be categorized by an equitable distribution of power between family and agency; one demonstration of this is the fact that the agency will almost always begin the relationship and necessarily defines when it will conclude. (Turnell & Edwards, 1997, p. 180)

Though we came to the practice of partnership via the brief therapy notion of cooperation, we quickly discovered that the concept is an evolving trend in the child protection field around the world. This trend toward partnership has been gathering momentum over the past decade, and there are very significant international developments that we will consider in the remainder of this chapter to set the context for a full exploration of our own approach.

The Voice of the Service Recipient
Begins to Be Heard

In the early 90s we went looking for research that documented the perspective of families that had been caught up in the child protection process. At that time such studies were hard to find. Magura and Moses (1984, p. 100) suggest that the views of "abusive" parents had been rarely sought due to the tendency to see them as "less capable, articulate and less objective than other human service recipients," and also the "considerable perceived difficulties of gaining their confidence" for research purposes.

Increasingly, however, during the 1990s the views of the service recipients have been sought out. Studies that we are now familiar with include Brown (1986), Corby (1987), Fryer, Bross, Krugman, Denson, and Baird (1990), MacKinnon (1992), Cleaver and Freeman (1995), Thoburn, Lewis, and Shemmings (1995), Farmer and Owen (1995), Winefield and Barlow (1995), and McCallum (1995). A deficiency of these studies is that the experiences and views of children and young people subjected to child protection investigations have largely been overlooked; notable exceptions to this are Farmer (1993) and Farmer and Pollock (1998).

The material in these studies does not make pretty reading, with service recipient's describing their experience of shock, fear, anger, humiliation, and resentment at the interventions they have experienced. These feelings are often long-lasting, and families consistently describe an overall sense of powerlessness in the face of child protection processes.

On a more positive note, the studies also conclude that when the worker showed an openness to the family's perspective, it was seen by parents as facilitating the development of a more cooperative and trusting relationship. MacKinnon found:

> professionals' skills in influencing parents' behavior, and the degree of their personal warmth and ability to develop a relationship characterized by respect and caring, were key factors in turning around situations that were otherwise perceived as negative by both parents and professionals. (1992, p. 298)

This was echoed in the research undertaken in Canada by McCallum, who found that:

> the interpersonal process between worker and parent is extremely important and is heavily influenced by the impressions conveyed by the worker to the parent. Conveyance of compassion, commitment and concern, along with respect, are regarded by parents as indicative of whether or not a worker can be trusted. This is facilitated by the skill of listening, careful use of self disclosure, and by workers being non-judgmental in regard to the family and its needs. (1995, p. 4)

Overall, consumer studies also convey the message that service recipients have a very accurate perception of whether the worker has a genuine interest in their views. Not surprisingly, families found it difficult to trust anyone who had the power to take control of their life. A positive relationship was more likely to develop when parents understood that the worker's focus was on the safety of the child(ren) in collaboration with the parents rather than safety for the child(ren) in opposition to the parents. Parents frequently felt that interviews focused too much on gathering evidence for the courts, and repeatedly asked to be treated as people rather than cases being dealt with "by the book."

One of the major factors working against engagement with families was the perceived emphasis placed on identifying deficits in family functioning and parenting. The focus on deficits and weaknesses, rather than strengths and resources, contributes to family defensiveness, which may be assessed as further evidence of resistance. The family's sense of its own capacities and capabilities can also be undermined by a steady stream of professionals focusing on what is wrong (Ban, 1992; Imber-Black, 1988; Pugh & De Ath, 1985). Service recipients also believed that if they were identified as "abusive parents" during the initial stages of contact with the agency it was difficult, if not impossible, to get workers to see them as capable parents at a later time.

In addition to these professional attempts to understand consumer views and experiences, service recipients have been proactive on their own behalf in influencing the child protection process, and organizations that represent them are becoming more vocal and assertive around the world. In the U.S., by the end of 1995, various advocacy groups acting on behalf of child protection service recipients had initiated litigation regarding inadequate child welfare services. Some of these actions have had significant outcomes, for example, in 1993 the American Civil Liberties Union undertook a legal challenge against the county of Milwaukee regarding the failure to provide services to children who were long-term wards. No professional had had contact with these children for up to four years. The U.S. district court found the state and the county equally culpable and, as a result, the state made the decision to take over the child protection services in that county, leading to a complete restructuring of the Milwaukee Human Services Department (McAllister, 1997). Whether this change will result in improved services to the recipients remains to be seen. However, it clearly highlights the impact that recipients can and do have on child protection practice.

The United Kingdom Experience: Cleveland and the 1989 Child Act

From the United Kingdom comes another scenario where professionals were taken to task by service recipients, the media, the government, and the general public, resulting in major changes in the child protection system. In 1987, child protection authorities in Cleveland removed 121 children from their families after each was medically diagnosed by two local pediatricians as having been sexually abused. The matter received enormous publicity within the United Kingdom and internationally. The initial media sentiment expressed horror at the alleged abuse. However, as the parents of the removed children mounted an active campaign of protest, media and public sentiment quickly turned to pillorying the social workers and doctors. A bitter and very public legal challenge ensued in the courts. When the court deemed 26 children from 12 families to have been wrongly diagnosed, the widespread view was that the professionals had been excessive and unjust in their intervention.

The Cleveland events created the momentum for a major overhaul of the child protection legislation in the United Kingdom, resulting in the 1989 Child Act. This legislation made partnership a central principle of child protection practice in that country and also triggered a comprehensive, research-based review of child protection practice involving 20 major research projects, including five based on studies involving service recipients. This work is summarized in the publication "Child Protection: Messages from Research" (Dartington Social Research Unit, 1995). The Cleveland scenario and what followed underlined the fact that child protection professionals cannot expect to act unilaterally; some level of collaboration and interaction is always necessary.

While the 1989 Child Act created partnership as a central concept for U.K. professionals and the notion inspired the politicians and bureaucrats, the question was soon asked: What do these fine words actually mean in practice? Morrison (1995, p. 133) pointed out that child protection workers are acutely aware "that any failure to protect children as a result of increased risk taking in the name of 'partnership' will be punished." The philosophy of partnership, while clearly important, raised the question: How is it to be implemented safely?

The New Zealand Experience and Family Group Conferences

At about the same time a somewhat similar process was evolving in New Zealand that resulted in another 1989 promulgation of legislation: the Children, Young Persons, and Their Families Act. Although it did not use the word partnership, this act enshrined the principle of family participation in decisions that affect their children. This development was also significantly influenced by service recipients. In this instance the pressure came from the Maori people (the native people of New Zealand), who had tired of the history of paternalism and the removal of their children. They demanded involvement of their traditional family and kinship groupings in the decision-making process when there were serious concerns about a child's welfare (Hassall, 1996).

The New Zealand act offered a crucial extra dimension that was lacking in the British equivalent: a partnership model of practice, namely family group conferences. The 1989 legislation requires that if, following investigation, a child is in need of care or protection, a family group conference must be convened. The family group conference is set up so that the extended family and others who the family wishes to attend are presented with the professional's concerns regarding the child's safety. This group then deliberates in private to arrive at a plan for the care and protection of the child. Family group conferences are prefaced on the assumption that families are competent to make decisions, rather than the more traditional notion that they are "pathological," "dysfunctional," or "deficient," and "are aimed at promoting effective functioning in families by focusing on their unique strengths and by enlisting them in a problem-solving process" (Hudson, Morris, Maxwell, & Galaway, 1996, p. 3).

The New Zealand initiative is arguably the most comprehensive practical implementation of partnership the international child protection field has yet seen. The family group conferencing model—minus the associated legislation—has attracted considerable attention and has been experimented with and utilized in many places around the world, with varying degrees of success. (See, for example, two 1996 edited volumes by Morris & Tunnard and Hudson et al.)

The U.S. Experience

There is certainly considerable service recipient pressure being brought to bear on child protection agencies in the U.S., in similar fashion to the Milwaukee legal action mentioned earlier. However, the evolution of partnership ideas and implementation has not come about in the U.S. through legislative processes; rather, the development has been more fragmented and confined to situations and agencies (both statutory and nonstatutory) that for one reason or another have become interested in this trend.

Several leaders in the brief therapy tradition, particularly John Weakland, Lynn Jordan, and Insoo Kim Berg, have been instrumental in developing child protection approaches that are based on the notion of cooperation between professionals and families. We have already mentioned the work of Weakland and Jordon (1990), and Insoo Kim Berg's general ideas are published in a book titled *Family-Based Services* (1994). Berg has also developed her work further and in recent years has been implementing what she calls a solution-building approach to child protection with the state child protection agency in Michigan (Berg & Kelly, forthcoming).

For four or five years the family group conference model has attracted considerable attention in the U.S. and various states have considered implementing this approach as a mechanism for developing partnership. A recent review of progress in this regard suggests that there are currently at least 25 states with active, well-planned family group conferencing initiatives, though even the most advanced are in the early stages of implementation (Merkel-Holguin, 1998).

Another model of child protection has evolved in the U.S. that is premised on increasing partnership with families, devolving responsibility for child safety away from the exclusive domain of professionals, and fostering wider community involvement. This approach has been given the name "community partnerships for protecting children" (Farrow, 1996). Iowa is one of the first states to begin to implement this approach, which incorporates assessment processes that allow for differential responses in services and "places less emphasis on the specific incident and greater emphasis on the family's strengths and concerns and developing a plan of action with the family" (The Center for Study of Social Policy, 1996, p. 2). Once again, it is interesting to note that the changes in Iowa were brought about by "outspoken parents (who) felt victimized by a system that labeled them as perpetrators" (The Center for Study of Social Policy, 1996, p. 2). Like family group conferencing, the community partnerships approach is certainly part of the world trend toward partnership, but the implementation of the model is in its infancy and it is too early to gauge its level of success.

THE PERSPECTIVE OF THE CHILD PROTECTION WORKER

It is our experience that, given the chance, child protection workers want to pursue partnership. When we train child protection workers, we will usually ask them to think of the best child protection worker they have encountered, someone whose work they would aspire to emulate. We ask them to list attributes of this worker. Consistently, field-based practitioners describe workers who are able to listen to and build a relationship with the people with whom they work and who also exercise their statutory authority with honesty and clarity. They always mention humanity and an ability to connect with clients. One African-American child protection worker of considerable experience captured this well when she said of the worker who inspired her, "Honey, she just treated every child as if it were her own!"

It is our contention that partnership between professional and family is not only something service recipients want but also what workers aspire to. If we are correct, this means there is a fit between the expectations and hopes of the two groups. This view was further confirmed for us when we heard about the development of Oregon's family group decision-making model, called family unity meetings (Graber, Keys, & White, 1996). In 1989, an audit of casework was being undertaken in the State Office for Services to Children and Families to which caseworkers exhibited considerable resistance. Graber, Keys, and White describe that "a dramatic change in the attitude on the part of the caseworkers" occurred when "the audit shifted from looking at problems to asking workers for their best thinking on how to help families" (p. 182). At this point, the workers "lined up to participate" and the ideas they offered resulted in the development of the family unity meeting model. The Oregon model has many similarities with family group conferencing but developed independently of it. The premises for good practice proposed by the workers, upon which the model is based, include the following:

- Respect and trust should be displayed to the family, and the family's point of view should be utilized wherever possible.
- Cooperation between the workers and the family should be developed from the outset.
- An emphasis should be placed on building the strengths of the family.

Interestingly, the audit also surveyed service recipients, asking them what they most valued. "They mentioned workers who listened, cared about them, believed in them, respected them, noticed their strengths, trusted them and didn't give up on them" (p. 183). This example, local to Oregon, demonstrates that what clients want even under the pressure of an intense child protection investigation does indeed dovetail with workers' best thinking. This, in our view, is a first-class example of a child protection agency closing Thomas's trench between the theoreticians (the auditors) and the workers. This in turn served as a parallel process to bridging the gap between workers and families.

CONCLUSION

It is apparent to us that families and workers are not that far apart regarding the sort of child protection system they want. The challenge is to create a structure and models of child protection practice that address the seriousness of alleged or substantiated maltreatment while maximizing the possibility of collaboration between families and workers. A child protection system that endlessly escalates professional authority and expertise is a recipe for paternalism. That is "more of the same" and, in our view, will only make the overall system worse. We have provided an overview in this chapter of attempts from around the world to implement a more collaborative approach between the professionals and service recipients.

It is important to recognize that models that implement partnership are not some sort of panacea or quick fix. The issues that are being dealt with in child protection are very serious and often life threatening for the children involved. It requires clarity of thinking, a certain amount of courage, and a gracefulness of touch for professionals to successfully collaborate with families. Workers cannot do it on their own; they require organizational backing as well as conceptual frameworks and models of practicing child protection that offer the necessary skill base to systematically build partnership.

The signs of safety approach offers such a framework, allied with corresponding skills, that fits the model squarely within the philosophy of partnership. The signs of safety approach is designed to be used from the first stage of gathering information about an allegation through case closure, and because of this it has broader applicability than the more narrowly focused conferencing models of partnership. The next chapter provides a thorough exploration of the principles that underpin the signs of safety approach, before we look at its application to each stage of the child protection process.

CHAPTER TWO

Practice Principles
That Build Partnerships

RESPECT SERVICE RECIPIENTS AS
PEOPLE WORTH DOING BUSINESS WITH

How we think about issues of child maltreatment will, not surprisingly, determine how we respond. For example, the taxi driver's thinking about parents who maltreat their children is, "There's nothin' you can do for them," and therefore the only thing that can be done is "to lock 'em up."

The taxi driver's position represents, explicitly but crudely, a version of paternalism suggesting that families where child maltreatment occurs cannot change or be trusted in any way. Therefore, the only hope is to be found in the intervention of the authorities. It is impossible to engage in a partnership with parents if one's underlying view is essentially akin to that of the taxi driver.

This chapter articulates some of the thinking—described here as practice principles—that guides the implementation of the signs of safety approach. Underpinning all of the practice principles is an attitude of respect toward the individuals who are the service recipients in the child protection process. Others, for example those charged with disseminating the messages from research findings in the United Kingdom (mentioned in the previous chapter) and those seeking to implement the family group conferencing model in various parts of the world (e.g., Ryburn & Atherton, 1996), have recognized that the attitude of professionals is a crucial ingredient in the successful implementation of a partnership-aspiring approach to child protection. The attitude that is required is one that in essence

29

TABLE 2.1
Practice Principles That Build Partnerships

1. Respect service recipients as people worth doing business with.

   Maintaining the position that the family is capable of change can create a sense of hope and possibility. Be as open-minded toward family members as possible, approaching them as potential partners in building safety.

2. Cooperate with the person, not the abuse.

   Workers can build a relationship with family members without condoning the abuse in any way. Listen and respond to the service recipient's story. Give the family choices and opportunities to give you input. Learn what they want. The worker must be up front and honest, particularly in the investigation. Treat service recipient as individuals.

3. Recognize that cooperation is possible even where coercion is required.

   Workers will almost always have to use some amount of coercion and often have to exercise statutory power to prevent situations of continuing danger, but this should not prevent them from aspiring to build a cooperative partnership with parents. Recognize that coercion and cooperation can exist simultaneously, and utilize skills that foster this.

4. Recognize that all families have signs of safety.

   All families have competencies and strengths. They keep their children safe, at least some, and usually most, of the time. Ensure that careful attention is given to these signs of safety.

5. Maintain a focus on safety.

   The focus of child protection work is always to increase safety. Maintain this orientation in thinking about the agency and the worker's role as well as the specific details and activities of the casework.

TABLE 2.1
Continued

6. Learn what the service recipient wants.

Acknowledge the client's concerns and desires. Use the service recipient's goals in creating a plan for action and motivating family members to change. Whenever compatible, bring client goals together with agency goals.

7. Always search for detail.

Always elicit specific, detailed information, whether exploring negative or positive aspects of the situation. Solutions arise out of details, not generalizations.

8. Focus on creating small change.

Think about, discuss, and work toward small changes. Don't become frustrated when big goals are not immediately achieved. Focus on small, attainable goals and acknowledge when they have been achieved.

9. Don't confuse case details with judgments.

Reserve judgement until as much information as possible has been gathered. Don't confuse these conclusions with the details of the case. Remember that others, particularly the family, will judge the details differently.

10. Offer choices.

Avoid alienating service recipients with unnecessary coercion. Instead, offer choices about as many aspects of the casework as possible. This involves family members in the process and builds cooperation.

11. Treat the interview as a forum for change.

View the interview as the intervention, and therefore recognize the interaction between the worker and the service recipients to be the key vehicle for change.

TABLE 2.1
Continued

12. Treat the practice principles as aspirations, not assumptions.

Continually aspire to implement the practice principles, but have the humility to recognize that even the most experienced worker will have to think and act carefully to implement them. Recognize that no one gets it right all the time in child protection work.

says "these are people worth doing business with" rather than "these are people we do business to."

Put simply, then, it should be apparent that the signs of safety model and the broader philosophy of partnership are underpinned by a measure of hope: hope that by working together things can be made safer for the family's children. However, given that child protection work involves situations where children are at risk of serious injury and, possibly, death, it is absolutely imperative that this sense of hope and attitude of respect and possibility are not confused with or transformed into naive practice. Dale et al. (1986) have described the naive practice of "professional dangerousness," where workers and their supervisors gloss over allegations of maltreatment and too readily accept parents' explanations, even implausible explanations about alleged or substantiated maltreatment, to ensure that the relationship with the family is not damaged. Similarly, Dingwall, Eekelaar, and Murray (1983) have described a phenomenom they call the "rule of optimism," wherein workers place their hope in simplistic solutions to address issues of maltreatment and thereby overlook minor injuries in children that may well be part of a pattern of increasing harm.

The hope and belief that working together can make things better and safer for the child is completely different from automatically or too quickly believing parents in a family where a child has been maltreated. Believing that individuals in families dealing with issues of abuse or neglect are worth doing business with is not at all the same thing as adopting the easiest way of doing business with them.

We are firm believers that building partnerships with families is the best way to protect vulnerable children, but we also know that building partnerships with parents and families in situations of child maltreatment is hard work that requires careful, thorough, and thoughtful practice. We believe that the signs of safety approach provides a way of thinking and of practicing child protection that enables a clear-eyed focus on danger and harm, while also fostering a context where the worker can be open-minded and respectful to family members, approaching them as potential partners in building safety. Below, we describe some practice principles that enable the worker to utilize the signs of safety model.

COOPERATE WITH THE PERSON, NOT THE ABUSE

A discordant relationship between the statutory worker and the family is unlikely to be fertile ground for creating change. Very few people will listen to or allow themselves to be influenced by someone who seems unresponsive to them and is simply forcing them to conform. The best chance to foster change within a family, whether there is maltreatment of children therein or not, is to build cooperative relationships with it members. As Perlman has said, "No matter what the theoretical model by which one human being attempts to be of help to another, the most potent and dynamic power for influence lies in the relationship" (1972, p. 150). However, for many child protection workers, the idea of cooperating with families where maltreatment is alleged or has occurred raises the immediate question: If I am responsive and cooperative with parents who are or might have been abusive, am I not signaling my acceptance of the violence? What needs to be achieved is a position of addressing the abuse while at the same time being receptive to the people involved: hence we propose the following maxim: Cooperate with the person, not the abuse.

It is usually not difficult to conceive of or build cooperation with the voluntary client. In child protection, however, not only are the clients usually involuntarily involved with the professional, but the situation is further complicated by the fact that it is usually the professional and the organization s/he represents that are adding to the problem for the client. The problem raised by the professional is also no small matter: telling parents that in some way or other their parenting is unacceptable. Within the helping professions there is probably no environment that puts the objective of building cooperation to the test more than that of child protection casework. So, while the notion of building a cooperative relationship can be seen as the best way to proceed and the most likely to generate change, the question arises: How can it be achieved?

To answer this question, we believe it is vital to return to the research that has been conducted with child protection service recipients, since these studies tell us what service recipients themselves want. The following summarizes the key aspects for building a cooperative relationship in child protection casework that we have distilled from these studies:

- First, and most importantly, parents and children want to be cared about as individuals and to have their strengths acknowledged as well as their weaknesses understood. Service recipients do not want to be treated as "another job lot," to use Cleaver and Freeman's (1995) phrase. This point comes across without exception in all the research.
- Allied to this, service recipients want to know that their story and their perspective regarding the allegations or incidents have been heard and understood.
- It makes a significant difference to families if the worker is responsive and sensitive to the turmoil and stress that the child protection process places on the family, especially in the early stages of the investigation.
- The contact between the statutory agency and the family should be based on honesty, with workers providing clear, straightforward information about who they are, why they have come to talk to the family members, what the allegations are, and what actions the agency might or will take at each step of the child protection process. Regular and full exchange of information throughout the life of the case is crucial to service recipients.
- The worker/agency should be explicit with the family regarding what it expects from them, rather than just focusing on what they have done wrong.
- The family wants to be listened to regarding their wishes and the ideas they have to improve the situation.
- Opportunities and structures should exist in the child protection process that allow the family to influence decisions and planning. The family is given choices regarding different options and the casework "takes account of their [the parents' and, where possible, the children's] views and incorporates their goals into plans" (Farmer & Owen, 1995, p. 322).

These, then, are very clear and specific aspects of practice that service recipients themselves say make a difference in the child protection relationship and are therefore fundamental for the worker seeking to build a cooperative relationship with the family.

RECOGNIZE THAT COOPERATION IS POSSIBLE, EVEN WHERE COERCION IS REQUIRED

At the end of the day, the statutory child protection agency has a societal and legal mandate to ensure the protection and safety of children. Therefore, as we have already indicated, limits exist in the manner in which cooperation can be developed, and there will also very clearly be times when the agency is unable to cooperate with specific perspectives and wishes of the family. Where indicators of harm and danger outweigh signs of safety, statutory intervention may well be required, and this will always be part of the child protection role. We want to emphasize that we do not wish to undermine the capacity of child protection services to exercise authority. We do, however, seek to have this authority exercised in a skillful manner.

Child protection professionals cannot successfully build partnerships by trying to pretend that they are in an equal relationship with service recipients. It is a simple fact that the child protection worker will always be the more powerful person in the relationship. They have the authority of the state behind them, they are able to remove the child and take other equally powerful courses of action, they usually define when the relationship begins, and they certainly hold most of the strings regarding when the relationship will end. These factors are not characteristic of an equitable relationship.

Surprising as it may seem, we firmly believe that a cooperative relationship is attainable between worker and family *even* when statutory intervention occurs and/or other forms of coercion are used. MacKinnon and James (1992a) offer a useful comment regarding these matters when they say:

> The exercise of coercion by those mandated to intervene in family violence appears to be a necessary aspect of protecting the vulnerable and creating leverage for change. Unless coercion is used in a considered and skillful fashion, however, it is likely to reinforce the very beliefs that allow an abusive parent to maintain violence as an option. (pp. 175–6)

This quote summarizes well the dilemmas faced by the statutory worker and also offers a way forward. Echoing MacKinnon and James, we believe that for child protection casework to be successful, the professional must be comfortable with the authority attached to the statutory role and be able to use that authority in a "considered and skillful fashion." Therefore, we adopt a both/and position (Lipchik, 1993), suggesting that the professional clearly yet sensitively take on the position of power and authority *and*, at the same time, do everything he or she can to build a cooperative relationship with the family under investigation. Although this is a big demand, we know from experience that it is achievable even in very serious and difficult child protection cases. We have seen workers do exactly this in many cases, and in the following chapters we will provide examples of how this has been achieved.

RECOGNIZE THAT ALL FAMILIES HAVE SIGNS OF SAFETY

Very often, child protection investigations become totally dominated by the issue of the maltreatment and associated risk factors, and assessments are made based on a "laundry list of all the things that are wrong with the client" (Berg, 1994, p. 17). When professionals get caught in thinking and talking about the families they work with in this way, the picture becomes very bleak and black-and-white. George Thomas (1995), drawing on many years' child welfare experience in the U.S. argues that, by this process, professionals overlook "95% of the behavior that may fall within broad definitions of ordinary competency and social acceptability while concentrating all the attention on the 5% identified to be problematic" (p. 20). Referring specifically to delinquent children, he talks of his own casework experience, saying, "Directing 100% of my attention to roughly 5% of these boys' behavior was the worst investment I ever made" (p. 21). Thomas goes on to say that "the one-sided focus on the problems converts whole people (parents and children) into problems, which prepares them for pigeonholing as cases arranged by case statuses" (p. 23).

This reduction of whole people into problems and case statuses severely undermines hope, the attitude of respect we talked of, as well the worker's capacity to see the individual person with whom to build cooperation. While not wanting to get caught up in an argument about the exact percentages Thomas uses, we definitely join him in calling child protection workers to direct a healthy amount of their attention to the "ordinary competency" of family strengths and resources and their importance as factors that may reduce the risks and balance the equation. The signs of safety approach proposes that every family has strengths, resources, their own way of solving problems, and their own goals. These are the signs of safety.

Here are a few shorthand examples of signs of safety from cases we have been involved with. In each case the behavior served to balance the danger/safety equation just a little:

- A mother who didn't know "the truth" in a situation where her husband had denied sexual abuse allegations of children outside the family nevertheless acted on the seriousness of the allegations by making sure her own children were not left alone with her husband.
- A man who sexually abused his stepdaughter confessed to his actions even while maintaining it was not his fault. He did this to save the child the trauma of having to face giving evidence in court.
- A drug-addicted mother separated from her addicted partner in an endeavor to clean up her life and regain custody of her children.
- A mother who had a history of becoming overwhelmed by depression and, as a consequence, would regularly get "blind drunk" for days at a time, thereby neglecting her children, resisted the urge to repeat this behavior on the anniversary of the death of one of her children and focused instead on activities with the two children in her care.

We are not saying such signs of safety guarantee absolute safety for the child, simply that they exist in each family. In families where children are maltreated, they are, after all, usually not being abused or neglected all the time. Therefore, there are many times when the family does provide a safe and "good enough" environment for the child. To work effectively with a family, it is invaluable for the worker to be able to elicit these aspects of family experience and functioning. These signs of safety provide a balance to the problems and dangers and provide many clues for developing a cooperative relationship with the family and for the development of appropriate, case-specific plans and interventions.

MAINTAIN A FOCUS ON SAFETY

If we were to conceive of the endeavor of child protection as a playing field, the goal posts would be clearly inscribed in large letters with the word SAFETY. Unfortunately, as consumer research suggests and as caseworkers who reflect on the vast bulk of the material contained within case files know, the professional child protection game frequently gets bogged down far from the goal, defeated by the laundry list of everything that is wrong and the 5% problematic behavior. Farmer and Owen (1995, p. 113) confirm this in their research of 120 child protection case conferences, where they found that the "preoccupation with risk meant there was simply too little time—nine minutes on average—to consider the needs of the family or what should be done." It is difficult to build partnership and cooperation if the primary focus of the casework stays on the problem and all that is wrong with the family in question.

The heart of the signs of safety approach is a focus on goals, namely, what the statutory agency needs to see to close the case as well as the family's ideas and ways of creating safety. This is exactly what we mean by focusing on safety, not as an avoidance of the issue of danger and harm, but as a mechanism for finding a way forward that will resolve the problems. Addressing the child protection risks through a purposive and careful focus on goals can readily create a context where cooperation is much more likely.

A very specific way for the worker to operationalize a focus on goals and safety is to develop the practice of talking about presence rather than absence. It is difficult and sometimes counterproductive in creating change to ask someone to simply *stop* something. It is usually more productive to help people *start* something. It is important, therefore, to tell the mother of a neglected child that she needs to be within eyesight or earshot of her baby at all times, and that she must put a lock on the garden gate. In a situation of sexual abuse it is better to ask a family to describe specifically how they intend to keep the older brother either apart from the younger sister he has sexually abused, or under adult supervision, during school vacation (inviting the family's ideas of the presence of safety), instead of simply asserting that he cannot be alone with his sister during the holidays (demanding the absence of something).

The notion that safety is the goal will be repeated time and again throughout this book. When the worker and family can focus attention on where they are trying to go, it is much more likely that both parties will actually get there, and furthermore, they are also more likely to be able to recognize when they have arrived.

LEARN WHAT THE SERVICE
RECIPIENT WANTS

A lot of attention in child protection is given to the issue of motivation. Workers often try to assess whether family members are motivated to change, and, often enough, service recipients are judged as lacking motivation. However, when approached in the right way, it is inevitable that families will reveal their own goals. Therefore, we seek in part to deal with the issue of motivation by paying attention to what motivates family members, rather than simply measuring their level of motivation in terms of professional conceptions of the problem and the solution. Hence, we think it is useful for workers to constantly ask themselves: Who's a customer for what?

It is rare in child protection that a family and agency see things in the same way in terms either of the problem or of the solutions. When workers become caught up in trying to get family members to see it their way, difficulties can quickly ensue. In child protection casework, the statutory agency has its own goals and will always be a customer for the goal of increased safety for the child. Whether the parents understand and are customers to the details of safety the agency outlines is another issue again. If both the family and the statutory agency share the goals of safety, they are both clearly customers for the same things, and a joint plan of action can readily be developed. If not, statutory action may be indicated. However, different motivations can be brought together. For example, the family may be a customer for the goal of "getting the child protection worker out of its hair," and from that perspective be willing to do some things to prove their child is safe just to "get rid of the worker." Here, a customer relationship exists, but by means of a different goal on the family's part. The agency might cooperate with the family's goal of getting rid of the worker, since it may fit with its own explicitly safety-focused goals.

In talking about who is a customer for what, we are drawing on a way of thinking that has been developed within the brief therapy tradition concerning client motivations and the relationship that exists between professional and service recipient. It is common in brief therapy (e.g., see Berg, 1994) to consider the relationship with the client in the following three ways:

- *Customer relationship:* Here there is agreement between the worker and the family regarding the problem, and the client is willing to do something to solve the problem.
- *Complainant relationship:* Again there is agreement between the worker and the family regarding the problem. However, while the clients complain about the problem, they are unwilling to do anything about it, perhaps because they feel that they are unable to or that it is not their responsibility.
- *Visitor relationship:* Here family members insist they do not have a problem and are certainly unwilling to do anything.

This way of thinking links client motivation to the nature of the relationship between the worker and the service recipient. In contrast, many models of child protection casework consider motivation as an attribute inherent in the client, completely overlooking the role of the worker, the impact of the relationship between professional and service recipient, and the importance of timing in broaching different issues.

For example, asking a mother at the end of an intensive investigatory interview, during which she has learned that her child is to be removed from her care, "What are your best ideas for making your child safer so that we can consider returning him to your care?" is likely to generate only a blank look from a woman who is feeling completely overwhelmed. From this response, the worker could form the view that, since the mother has no ideas and is displaying little interest in the child's safety, she is unmotivated to change. On the other hand, the worker who comes back to that same mother a few days later, talks carefully and slowly about what has happened, and then asks the same question is likely to get a completely different and more receptive response from the mother. This may seem an exaggerated and obvious example, but in our experience it is amazing how frequently workers underestimate the amount of stress their intervention creates and also misjudge a service recipient's sense of powerlessness to be a lack of motivation.

We believe that motivation is an attribute that should be talked about in the context of the relationship between the worker and service recipient, not regarded as a residual characteristic of the client. This also allows recognition that motivation will ebb and flow relative to many factors and that the worker and agency share a professional responsibility to create a context that maximizes the likelihood of family members displaying their motivation.

An example that we will discuss in more detail in chapter 8 highlights this. In this case the father had been jailed for sexual abuse of the mother's niece. After his release the statutory agency was very frustrated because the mother seemed to be ambivalent about her own daughter's safety. For her part, the mother felt frustrated that the agency wanted her to do still more when, in her view, she was the one who had already received the brunt of the punishment. Suffering from severe health problems, she had been thrown into poverty by the imprisonment and had been left with the sole care of three young children. Moreover, her own family had ostracized her because of the actions of her spouse. When her experience was acknowledged by a new worker, she began to collaborate with the agency's concerns.

This woman was, in the first instance, a customer for having the sacrifices she had made and hardship she had endured recognized by the authorities. The worker who paid attention to this and did not judge her to be unmotivated (a judgment that would have been particularly offensive in the light of all she had dealt with and done) laid the foundation for significant change. Throughout this book we will present examples of child protection workers who through careful work have had a significant impact on the motivation of service recipients. Asking "who is a customer for what?" is one way of encouraging workers to be open-minded about what the service recipients might want and to broaden their perspective to include those desires along with the agency's needs.

ALWAYS SEARCH FOR DETAIL

The success of any child protection investigation and subsequent casework will in large part be determined by the amount and quality of detailed information the worker is able to elicit. Whether discussion with a family focuses on the maltreatment (alleged or substantiated), family history, strengths, resources, or goals, the worker should *always search for detail!* It is important to know not only that the child was hit, but also what led up to this, who else was involved, and what happened afterwards. When a complaint of abuse is taken over the telephone from a third party, it is necessary to know how the complainant knows about the abuse, what he or she has actually witnessed, and the context of the event(s). There is a long tradition of tracking meaningful detail regarding the problem and interactions associated with it in the literature of the brief therapy field (for example, see Cade & O'Hanlon, 1993, pp. 49–63, and Fisch et al., 1982, pp. 69–78). Since this attention to detail has considerable application to interviewing in child protection, we recommend that workers familiarize themselves with this material.

Likewise, in pursuing signs of safety—strengths and resources, goals, and exceptions to the problems—the more detailed the discussion, the greater the usefulness of the information. It is somewhat useful to know that a father can think of one time when he could have readily maltreated his child and didn't, but it is more valuable to know when, where, and how he was able to do that, what others might have noticed was different about him, and how *he* understands what he did. When an initial phone complaint about neglect is received, it is important to gain detailed information about the complaint, and it will also be valuable to find out from the complainant the "who, what, where, and when" of situations when the parents *are* appropriately responsive to the child's needs.

At the beginning of this chapter we considered the issues of "professional dangerousness" and casework guided by the "rule of optimism." Where the case worker elicits thorough and detailed information about family functioning, both negative and positive, from sources both inside and outside the family, this, perhaps more than any other activity, serves as a crucial antidote to naive practice. Quite simply, detailed information provides the best basis for realistic assessment and case plans.

FOCUS ON CREATING SMALL CHANGE

Radical economist Fritz Schumacher (1973) popularized the phrase "small is beautiful" in the field of economics. This credo is equally applicable to the field of child protection. It is important that child protection workers think small in terms of what they are trying to achieve. The brief therapy tradition that informs the signs of safety approach has always focused on small change, since it postulates that change is continuous and therefore one (small) change will inevitably lead to further change (e.g., Cade & O'Hanlon, 1993; Weakland et al., 1974).

The task of the child protection caseworker is made much easier if s/he thinks in terms of small changes. Sometimes workers or their agencies get bogged down because they are seeking an immediate case outcome that is altogether too big, often allowing the ultimate goal to overwhelm the exploration of smaller progress. For example, a case we will consider in detail in chapter 9 had become stuck because the agency was demanding that the mother immediately retake full parental responsibility for her teenage son. The new worker assigned to the case was able to begin making progress in the first face-to-face meeting by focusing on the mother's perspective and aiming to simply achieve a mutual discussion. Successfully accomplishing these small goals subsequently enabled the worker to enlist the mother in the further small goal of restarting the relationship with her son by phoning him at the institution where he was staying.

Frequently, trying to achieve big goals quickly leads only to frustration. It is usually more helpful for both the worker and the family if the focus is maintained on specific and small changes (Weakland & Jordan, 1990). In our experience, thinking small inevitably, but perhaps paradoxically, leads cases to resolution more quickly, even if only for the reason that everyone involved is more likely to have a sense that something is being achieved.

Yvonne Dolan, who specializes in working with clients who have experienced severe trauma and abuse, titled her latest book *One Small Step*. She contends that small changes pave the crucial pathway to larger ones: "Approaching cherished hopes and dreams one step at a time makes them less daunting and, most important, makes them undeniably achievable in real everyday life" (1998, p. 2).

DON'T CONFUSE CASE DETAILS
WITH JUDGMENTS

A child protection colleague* who surveyed a number of service recipients to gain their ideas regarding risk assessment was struck by the comment of a mother regarding the differences in perception she sensed between herself and the professional during the investigation. The woman stated: "If I had said my dog was blue, I would have meant it was sad, but they would have thought I painted it."

Child protection professionals must make judgments, and very significant ones at that: judgments about whether children should be separated from their parents, judgments that may leave children at risk, judgments that ultimately affect family life and that are crucial

---

*Julie Boffa, Department of Human Services Victoria, Australia.

to potentially vulnerable individuals. However, as the reflection of the service recipient and her "blue" dog highlights exquisitely, judgments are interpretations applied to information or events.

As we have seen, child protection casework traditionally operates on the assumption that the work is carried out from an "objective and professional" perspective where "expert knowledge" is attained from "the facts" and the judgments that professionals make are "the truth" about a situation. This perspective renders largely invisible the reality that it is simply one human being, or a group of human beings, with their own particular worldview, values, and beliefs making these judgments about other human beings. The family could not receive these labels without the professionals (with their particular perspectives and expertise) doing the labeling. As we have suggested in the earlier discussion regarding assessing motivation, the signs of safety approach emphasizes the interactional nature of the attribution of meaning. Further, the simple fact—which cannot, in our view, ever be overemphasized—is that what the statutory agency and its workers see and judge significant is often quite different from the perspective and priorities of the family.

A single mother, whose child has been taken into care, may be particularly sullen and uncommunicative when interviewed by a child protection worker. The mother may suddenly walk out of the office, abruptly ending the interview. A report regarding this interview may conclude that the mother is resistant, unmotivated, and not interested in working with the statutory agency. The mother's view of events and her judgment may be rather different: In the six months since her child was taken from her care she has become increasingly angry, first because of the many weeks that elapsed between the initial removal of her child and subsequent recontact (Farmer & Owen, 1995, found this to be a frequent service recipient complaint), and second because numerous different workers have been involved with her case. At the latest meeting she was interviewed by yet another new worker who asked questions very similar to those she had already answered repeatedly. Further, she has experienced numerous upheavals in the past week. For her, this new worker asking the same questions was the last straw and confirmed her own judgment that nothing was going to change, nobody would listen to her, and there was little she could do to make any difference—so she walked out.

In case conferences, the judgment is sometimes made that parents have no ideas regarding what should happen, because they are unable to suggest anything in these meetings. At other times, parents are thought to agree with a case plan because they raised no objections and thereby seemed to give their assent at the conference. Thoburn, Lewis, and Shemmings state that the most common complaint from child protection service recipients regarding case conferences was "They'd [the professionals] made up their minds before we came in, they weren't listening" (1995, p. 223). McCallum (1995) in her Canadian study, found that parents believed that once they were defined as unable to care for their children, there was no way they could redeem themselves. This clearly highlights that any child protection judgments attributed to passivity or resistance need to be made carefully.

Time and time again, we have seen that, for very good reasons (time pressures, large caseloads, the stress of relating to a particular individual, etc.), overly harsh judgments are made that do not necessarily fit the information and events. Perhaps conclusions are drawn on limited information and/or do not mesh with the views of the family or parents. This is not to say that parents and professionals must always agree on judgments, but we do believe good child protection practice will identify and be very responsive to differences in perception and judgment.

Our purpose here is neither to prescribe agreement in child protection judgments, nor to proscribe judgments. Rather, drawing on the ideas of Cade and O'Hanlon (1993) we want to emphasize what we consider to be a critical distinction between events and information, on the one hand, and the meanings and judgments that are ascribed to those events and information, on the other. The distinction may be a simple one, but it can have a profound impact on assessment and casework. It is not uncommon for the two to become entangled in child protection discussions and documentation and for file notes to be written as if certain events definitively demonstrate certain judgments. Once a judgment is made, there is a tendency not to gather any more information or material regarding the judged events, and further information is often processed in the light of the previous judgment. Cicchinelli and Keller (cited in English & Pecora, 1994) found that, although risk assessment is promoted as an information-gathering and decision-making tool, it often serves to verify or document decisions already made.

Judgments, therefore, will often direct how the caseworker interacts with the family. For example, if, in the case of a man who regularly beats his child, the worker concludes (ascribing a judgment to the fact of the beatings) that this man is incapable of resolving difficulties in any other manner than using violence, it is unlikely that the worker will ask an exception question: "Are there times when you could have hit your child and didn't?" or "What other ways do you discipline your child?" To ask these sorts of questions requires some degree of open-mindedness on the part of the worker.

We encourage and train child protection workers to be continually mindful of the difference between events and information and their meanings. Further, we encourage workers to hold their judgments in abeyance as long as is realistically possible. When judgments are made, as they have to be, the chances of cooperation will be enhanced if these are held lightly and are made vulnerable to new information, particularly information relating to the service recipient's perspective.

OFFER CHOICES

Consumer research in child protection repeatedly tells us that when clients feel they have been given a say in matters and presented with options, they respond favorably (Brown, 1996; MacKinnon, 1992). Conversely, when they feel they are simply told what they must do, they become alienated from the process. A very simple and clear way of involving service recipients is to offer them choices wherever possible. This can begin from the very first contacts.

The idea of giving choice does not mean that workers collude with the abuse of children by, for example, giving the parents the final choice as to whether or not a child is removed from the family home. By offering choice wherever possible, we are seeking here to minimize the power differential between service recipient and professional, not eradicate it. The capacity to give choice does mean, however, that workers and the agency need to be clear about the nonnegotiable requirements and aspects of the case (Rooney, 1988).

For skillful workers, giving service recipients choice becomes part of the process of doing business, rather than an end in itself. Again, it is important to think small, and a little lateral thinking is also beneficial. For example, a family might be told "We need to discuss these issues with you today. Can you suggest the best time and place for us to meet during the day?" Families can be given a choice regarding who attends case conferences, whether they attend a parenting course, or which specific counselor they see. A family may even be given a choice to take 24 hours to demonstrate or come up with ideas to reduce risks and improve safety. This may defer the need for statutory action. One of our colleagues (this case will be discussed fully in chapter 7), after having informed the mother by phone that her child would have to be removed from her care, offered the choice of whether he and his fellow worker would come to the home with or without the police. Another colleague gave a mother the choice regarding who should conduct the investigatory interview with her husband, a stranger or an officer the husband already knew. In the Netherlands it is common practice for the investigating team to gather information about the allegation and then prepare a letter containing this information that is sent to the parents. The letter requests that the parents get in touch with the statutory agency as soon as they have been able to assimilate the information to arrange a meeting.

TREAT THE INTERVIEW AS A FORUM
FOR CHANGE

"The interview is the intervention" is a catch cry, popular among some therapists/caseworkers, that emphasizes that human face-to-face contact is what makes the most difference rather than grand interventions, strategies, or plans. As Jeffreys and Stevenson (1997, pp. 75–6) propose, even "child protection investigations can be therapeutic, and it is worth noting that they can develop a family's understanding of the issues, and offer support and education."

We are suggesting, therefore, that child protection caseworkers consider the interview as the primary intervention. This encompasses the way they ask questions, what questions they ask, how forthright and straightforward they are, the compliments given, the matching of the family's thinking and language, and everything else that goes to make up the interviews they have with the family. The case plan and interventions are icing on the cake. The personal contact in the interviews and meetings involving the worker and family is the setting in which the relationship develops. The interview is the intervention precisely because it is the relationship between the worker and the family that is the principal vehicle for change.

TREAT THE PRACTICE PRINCIPLES
AS ASPIRATIONS RATHER
THAN ASSUMPTIONS

We do not want the practice principles articulated in this chapter to be regarded as the assumptions on which the signs of safety model rests. We are wary of the notion of assumptions. To assume something too often implies taking something—in this case an idea—for granted. The ideas presented here as practice principles cannot and should not be taken for granted.

Marsh (1990) pointed out that when child welfare workers consider new ideas and practices there is a tendency for the DATA (Do All That Already) effect to come into operation. The ideas and principles we have presented lend themselves to this tendency because in some ways, as with the broader notion of partnership, they read like motherhood statements (i.e., at least at first glance, it's difficult to disagree with them). However, it is one thing to agree with the principles and ideas and it is quite another to put them into practice. In fact, we have not yet met the worker who has fully integrated these principles into his or her child protection practice such that s/he could confidently assert, "These are the assumptions upon which all my work is based."

It seems to us that paternalism, or what another writer calls "expertosis" (Smart, 1994), is essentially the helping professional's default setting. Under pressure—and child protection workers are often under considerable pressure—most of us in one way or another fall back on the position, "I'm the expert and you, the service recipient, need to listen and do what I say." We would, therefore, be suspicious of the professional who told us "I do all that already," since the practice principles, in our view, function as aspirations rather than assumptions. By this we mean that these principles serve as ideals of practice for the worker to aspire to. Professionals, whether new to the field or highly experienced, will always face challenges in applying them.

The practice principles will be continually revisited throughout the remainder of this book, particularly as we consider how child protection workers have applied them in practice. In the next chapter these principles are developed into the six practice elements of the signs of safety approach.

CHAPTER THREE

A Map of the Territory: The Six Practice Elements

Child protection workers who confront the difficulties and tensions of child maltreatment on a daily basis need a map to guide them through the challenging territory in which they work. Without a map or framework for their practice—especially in the interviews they conduct—it is all too easy for workers to get swamped by the myriad dynamics, stories, emotions, and reactions that are an inevitable part of child maltreatment situations.

The usual child maltreatment map revolves around gathering information about danger and harm. For the purposes of risk assessment, caseworkers usually collect information on factors such as the severity and pattern of the maltreatment, the perceptions of family members regarding abuse and neglect, the vulnerability of the child to future harm, the tendency toward violence within the family, and such additional factors as substance abuse, mental disorders, and any history of childhood abuse in the parents' lives (Sigurdson & Reid, 1996).

It is our contention that most risk assessment maps are too one-sided. Focusing attention exclusively on a family in the areas just mentioned is rather like mapping only the darkest valleys and gloomiest hollows of a particular territory. There can be no doubt that the child protection worker must gather information about past and potential harm and family deficiencies, but, to balance the picture, it is also vital to obtain information regarding past, existing and potential safety, competencies, and strengths. The six practice elements of the signs of safety model provide one map to assist the worker to elicit, amplify, and assess the constructive side of a family's capabilities. Explicitly and carefully considering both danger and safety in this way allows for a more comprehensive and balanced assessment of risk.

1. POSITION REGARDING THE PROBLEM, ITS SOLUTION, AND THE STATUTORY AGENCY

Each family member's story about the alleged maltreatment provides important information regarding both danger and safety. It is vital that the child protection worker listen to these stories and understand the *position* of each family member. By the term *position* we mean the strongly held values, beliefs, and meanings that individuals express through their stories. Acknowledging an individual's position is a fast and powerful way of quickly building understanding and rapport. This understanding will allow the worker to communicate with the family in its own language and facilitate the process of change. The notion of position was first articulated within the focused problem resolution model of brief therapy and traditionally focuses attention on the meanings that the individual attaches to the problem scenario (for further discussion see Fisch et al., 1982). It is crucial in successful family-professional collaboration to consider the service recipient's position regarding safety and possible solutions, as well as their position toward the worker and the statutory agency.

A recent case that shocked the Western Australian public highlights a dramatic example of one man's position regarding his perception of abuse. Following the death of his three-year-old stepson from a severe beating at his own hands, this man stated, "He doesn't like me. I don't know why. He grizzles. Why can't he just say, 'Good morning, Ken?' He never says it to me" (Fitzpatrick & Lang, 1996). In this tragic situation there was an extensive story of the sad events given by the stepfather to police, but what underpins it for this man is the belief "he doesn't like me and won't say 'good morning' and won't show respect/love for me." It is offensive that a man who has killed his stepson could adopt such a seemingly trivial position, and his perspective is a totally inadequate defense for what he has done. Nevertheless, working directly with this man will require understanding and engaging with his position and thinking.

TABLE 3.1
The Six Practice Principles

1. Understand the position of each family member.

   Seek to identify and understand the values, beliefs and meanings family members perceive in their stories. This assists the worker to respond to the uniqueness of each case and to move toward plans the family will enact.

2. Find exceptions to the maltreatment.

   Search for exceptions to problem. This creates hope for workers and families by proving that the problem does not always exist. Exceptions may also indicate solutions that have worked in the past. Where no exceptions exist, the worker may be alerted to a more serious problem.

3. Discover family strengths and resources.

   Identify and highlight positive aspects of the family. This prevents the problems from overwhelming and discouraging everyone involved.

4. Focus on goals.

   Elicit the family's goals to improve the safety of the child and their life in general. Compare these with the agency's own goals. Use the family's ideas wherever possible. Where the family is unable to suggest any constructive goals, danger to the child is probably increased.

5. Scale safety and progress.

   Identify the family members' sense of safety and progress throughout the case. This allows clear comparisons with workers' judgements.

6. Assess willingness, confidence, and capacity.

   Determine the family's willingness and ability to carry out plans before trying to implement them.

No two situations of child abuse are the same. The "facts" may be very similar, but the position, circumstances, and perceptions of each family are different and requires different responses. If workers can uncover the particular position of each relevant family member, it is more likely the worker will be able to show genuine understanding and find a way to establish collaboration. It is also more likely that realistic case plans, which fit with the family's perspective, will be achieved. It is important to underline that paying attention to an individual's position can be done without agreeing with or condoning their beliefs about the abuse or neglect.

Examples of positions regarding the problem that the child protection worker will frequently encounter include:

- He is such a disobedient and bad child, there is nothing else I could do.
- There is nothing wrong with what I did, it's simply do-gooders and nosey parkers who see it as wrong.
- We're doing the best we can to deal with him; its the ex-wife who keeps messing him up.
- I was hit and treated like this when I was a kid and I'm okay.
- I couldn't help what I did; it's all his fault!
- My husband could never do a thing like that to our daughter.
- Yeah okay, I admit how I treated my child was wrong.

It is also important to pay attention to the position family members hold regarding the statutory agency and its workers, such as the following:

- If I tell them the truth, I'll lose my child.
- They never listen to you: they're only interested in what they want to do.
- The workers aren't perfect, but they really do their best to help you.

When building safety, it is important to consider how individuals position themselves regarding possible solutions. For example:

- I'm helpless to do anything with her.
- This whole experience has cost me so much already, and nobody acknowledges what I've done, so I'm not doing anything more.
- I am exhausted from looking after my three children. There is no way I can keep my eye on them all the time.

- I don't need to talk about it. I just need some practical help.
- I was abused like her, and my mother never believed me when I told her. I'm going to make sure she knows I believe her.

Understanding position is equivalent to understanding the plot in a play or story: once you get it, the characters and the action tend to make much more sense. Once position is understood, the worker must consider how to utilize the knowledge. Dean and Locke (1983) offer a process they call "RATUG" for utilizing the positions of family members. They say:

> In our view, if a worker approaches any situation with the belief that he should RESPECT whatever a person and/or family is offering him, no matter how bizarre, mad or bad it may seem, then he is in a position to APPRECIATE that this is the best the person/family is able to do at this moment in time, i.e. they are offering the best they know rather than the worst. With this frame of mind the worker can TAKE what the person/family is offering and USE it to provide a GRACEFUL way out of the problem situation. (p. 98)

Case example

A middle-aged man was investigated regarding an allegation that he had sexually interfered with a 17-year-old overseas male student in his care. When interviewed, the man denied many of the events the teenager had clearly described, but did admit to others, which he explained as "sex education." The man vehemently refuted suggestions that he had molested the boy and claimed he was responding to a request from the boy to assist him after the young man had undergone a circumcision. The man claimed the boy had misconstrued his "practical" approach as an invitation for sexual activity and accused the boy of making up the allegations because he wanted to change hosts to avoid further difficulties regarding issues such as borrowing money and unauthorized social activities.

The agency was of the opinion that there was insufficient evidence to take legal action in the situation, but it was agreed that some action needed to be taken. The worker returned to see the man and initiated a discussion with him regarding his position on "sex education." In this conversation the man acknowledged that should his "practical" methods be submitted for approval to the governing host body and the parents of students, others might also construe the incidents in exactly the way the boy did. This could be embarrassing and damage his reputation as a businessman and as a host parent. Following this, the man agreed to cooperate with the boy's desire to change hosts and to deregister himself as a host parent for any students under the age of 18 years.

In this case, utilizing the man's own position led to a collaborative solution and a safe outcome for the boy. It is questionable whether the same results could have been achieved through contested legal or administrative processes.

Position Regarding Safety and the Statutory Agency

Being responsive to a parent's position in no way means that statutory action is precluded. It is possible to both prosecute a father on an assault charge for severely beating his daughter with a belt, as well to connect with him regarding his feelings of frustration and powerlessness over a rebellious adolescent who has involved a younger sibling in drug-taking and other criminal activities. Engaging the father in this way may well elicit a history of past attempted, yet unsuccessful, solutions: consultations with pediatricians, family therapy, regular contact with the school counselor, and even sending the teenager to stay with relatives overseas in an attempt to let the extended family and its culture influence her. Understanding these efforts allows the worker more insight into the man's frustration. The worker can compliment the father on his determination, while avoiding attempts to persuade him to undertake actions that have already been unsuccessful.

In another case, a young father was successfully prosecuted—as he needed to be, since there was clear evidence of assault occasioning bodily harm—for severely burning his very young son when he doused the child's foot in kerosene and then set it aflame. The burn was far more severe than the father had intended, but he admitted his actions, explaining his "position" that his son needed to be taught a lesson for lighting dangerous fires in the family home. The case was exclusively dealt with in a legal fashion, and it is uncertain what the father has learned from the process. If a professional was to discuss this matter with the young father, it would not be difficult for the worker to agree with the father's position (that the child must be punished to teach him a lesson about dangerous behavior) and then carefully explore with him more appropriate ways of disciplining his son.

This scenario also highlights the fact that service recipients have their own position regarding solutions and plans of action. Hopefully, in the case just mentioned (and it was surely part of the aim of the court), the man has changed his position regarding appropriate responses to his son's misbehavior. Whenever exploring solutions, it is important to consider how family members position themselves regarding plans for building safety.

It is also important that the professional consider the position and beliefs service recipients hold regarding the statutory agency and the worker. In 1997 we published an article on the signs of safety approach that began with the popular joke: "What is the difference between a rottweiller and a social worker?" The answer: "Sometimes you can get the rottweiller to let go of your child." Some professionals voiced their disapproval of our using such a seemingly disrespectful joke to commence our paper. Our point, though, was to emphasize that this is a very common community perception or position regarding child protection workers. In fact, without that common perception, the joke would have no currency. Since these perceptions regarding child protection professionals are widespread, workers must proceed carefully in building their relationship with a family. In this regard, it is worth remembering that Farmer and Owen (1995) found that many service recipients resolutely believed that because of the intrusiveness of the initial investigation, particularly where children were removed, it was impossible for them to cooperate with the original investigative worker(s).

The following questions provide avenues for exploring the position of family members.

Regarding the problem:

- From the report, you can see how others view things. What is your perspective on this situation?
- How would you describe what is happening in your family as a result of this issue?
- How is this a problem for you?
- How do you make sense of what he does?
- How do you explain what you did?
- How do you think your son would explain what happened?

Regarding solutions and plans:

- Why do you think that course of action would be most helpful?
- What makes you think that these plans won't make any difference?
- Some people might say you need to do _____ in this situation. What do you think about that?

- If we were to suggest that he do _____ (or that we will do ____),
  what would be the best way of explaining that to him/her?

  Regarding the worker and agency:

- How hopeful are you that I/we can be of assistance to you?
- I'm sure many people would say we're not interested in your
  opinions and what you want. Do you think that's true?

It is always useful for the worker to check his/her perception
against those of the family members. Therefore the following question can be beneficial:

- It seems to me that your opinion could be summarized as _____
  (insert position). Is that right?

Two case examples

A child protection worker was notified by phone of a situation where
two five-year-old children had been seriously sexually abused by an
11-year-old boy. The notification was made by a childcare worker
from the organization where the abuse had occurred. The childcare
worker's position was that the child protection authorities really
did not need to investigate the matter further since she had already
discussed the incidents with the older boy's mother, a health care
professional, who would deal with the matter. The childcare worker
also seemed to be concerned about the reputation of the center.

It would have been easy for the worker to become oppositional
with the caller and instigate a full investigation without the cooperation of the childcare worker. However, the child protection worker
dealt more sensitively with the childcare worker's position. First,
the worker invited the childcare worker to reflect on the seriousness
of the matter for the two five-year-olds and their parents. The
worker then acknowledged that the incidents could well have a
negative effect on the reputation of the center but asked her to
reflect on the much more serious consequences if it appeared that
the childcare center was trying to cover up the matter. The worker
also invited the caller to consider the consequence if it was discovered
that other children had also been abused. By asking these sorts of
questions, further exploring the child care worker's reflections and
position, the child protection worker skillfully enlisted the childcare
worker's cooperation in a full child protection investigation.

Obviously, some positions taken by service recipients are more indicative of safety and others more indicative of danger. However, workers cannot expect to convince every service recipient to adopt the correct, "safe" positions and beliefs. Approaching family members in this way is likely to generate more arguments than change. Assisting people to change their fundamental beliefs is certainly a very powerful way of generating change. However, this is not the only method, and it is not our primary purpose in identifying position as a key practice element. Whatever position a service recipient holds, we believe it is a sign of safety when the worker understands and is responsive to that perspective. This openness is a key element in building cooperation, and it is the cooperative relationship that we see as the principle vehicle for creating change and increasing safety.

It is frequently a challenge to discover how to work creatively and constructively with the service recipient's position. When cases become stuck it is often useful for workers to remember family members' positions and to reconsider their own position regarding the family and the maltreatment. When a worker becomes unmovable on an issue, he or she can easily lose sight of the flesh and blood people who are involved. Workers who forget this reality may impede the progress of the case.

In another case, a 13-month-old baby was removed from the care of its mother, a very recent European immigrant who came to Australia to marry the baby's father. The marriage lasted only a short time. The woman had been threatening to kill herself and the baby. She had been psychiatrically diagnosed with a bi-polar affective disorder and a borderline personality disorder, along with the assessment that she had poor impulse control. Her care of the child had been described as "erratic," "inappropriate," and, at times, "completely neglectful and inattentive." The child had been placed in the care of the father, and court action was pending to enable the statutory agency to take custody of the child, since there were also concerns regarding the father's capacity to care for the child. The worker* was trying, unsuccessfully, to build a collaborative relationship with the mother.

The social work supervisor suggested that the worker's position (that the mother was chaotic and severely mentally disturbed) was

---

*Joe Fleming

preventing him from considering her perspective. The worker accepted this feedback and made an effort to be more open-minded toward the mother. Specifically, he acknowledged those points that the mother had repeatedly asserted: there was indeed a bond between mother and daughter, and this was evident in the fact that the baby became distressed after the mother concluded access visits. He also acknowledged that the mother did have valid concerns regarding the safety of the child with the father, as she had been assaulted on more than one occasion by the man. The worker understood that relaxing his own position toward the mother was the crucial shift that enabled progress to be made in this case.

Where both service recipient and worker are able to acknowledge each other's position this is invaluable in building cooperation and is therefore a vital sign of safety.

2. EXCEPTIONS TO THE
ABUSE/NEGLECT

One example of an exception question is described in the introduction, asked of the abusive father by Insoo Kim Berg: "Have there been any times when you have been in a rage but resisted the urge to hit your daughter?" Such powerful questions are useful in stretching the worker's thinking and eliciting new information. Exceptions (originally described by Steve de Shazer, Insoo Kim Berg, and their colleagues in de Shazer et al., 1986) are times when the problem (in this instance, the abuse or neglect) could have happened but didn't.

A parent who had previously lashed out at her child described a situation where she had become enraged but resisted the impulse to hit the child by doing something else. The caseworker elicited the information by asking her to "tell me about the times when you get your child to listen to you without hitting her." This form of questioning is based on two assumptions: that the problem is not happening all the time and that the person probably deals appropriately with the problem some of the time. Exception questions can be particularly valuable in child protection work, as they allow discussion and acknowledgment of the problem in a constructive manner, without the need for confrontation.

Exception questions not only uncover the absence of negative behaviors, but are instrumental in discovering the presence of safe and constructive behaviors. It is important that, when the family member describes such behavior, the worker asks questions that assist in enlarging the description into a complete picture, including the "when, where, how, and what" of the incident. The greater the detail, the more valuable the information will be to all parties. It is also important to find out how confident the service recipient is in his/her ability to repeat the exception.

Exception questions tailored to each case can generate examples such as the following:

- A child described being able to go to her grandmother's home when she felt unsafe because her parents had become too drunk to care for her.
- A mother was able to deal "reasonably calmly" with her 3-year-old son after he had forced pieces of fruit into the VCR. In less aggravating situations she had previously "flown into a rage" and lashed out at the boy.
- A man who had previously assaulted his stepson resisted the urge to do so on another occasion, even though the teenager had thrown a knife at him. He did this by telling himself, "If I hit him, the boy will only make a monkey of me again."
- Another father resisted the urge to physically punish his son and instead dealt with the matter by taking the boy to the police to have him charged.
- A grandmother described a period where her drug-addicted daughter had faced up to her problems and acknowledged she was not caring adequately for her child. At that time the mother had sent the girl to live with her father for nine months while she detoxed herself.

Exception questions are invaluable at the intake stage. After the initial allegation has been made, the worker can ask the caller a question like, "Can you tell me about times when this parent has responded appropriately in keeping the child safe?" Any positive answer to this question will provide the investigative worker with a constructive avenue to explore existing safety at subsequent interviews.

On the other hand, a worker who asked the maternal grandmother "Can you tell about the times when your daughter's care of the child and her household management is okay?" received the adamant reply, "There are none; it never happens!" The completely negative nature of the woman's assertions began to alert the worker that this was probably an allegation motivated out of malice toward her daughter rather than genuine concern for her grandchild.

Some useful questions for exploring exceptions include:

- You said earlier on that it's not always like this. Can you tell me more about the other times?
- When was the last time this problem happened? How have you managed to avoid it since then?
- What was different about the times you felt like you handled the situation well?
- Have you been in this situation before? What did you do that helped?
- Can you tell me about times when this parent has responded appropriately in keeping the child safe? What did she do?
- Clearly, there are many times when you do keep track of your son even when you are tired. Can you tell me how you do that?
- When was the last time you felt you had the energy to care for your children well? How were you able to do that?

Interviewing with Sensitivity and Persistence

It is important to be mindful of the issue of timing in asking exception questions. Exception questions must build upon an acknowledgment of the allegation or at least of a problem scenario. Before the interviewee—whether a family member or another professional—will readily discuss exceptions, they need to feel they have been understood. The worker must also be aware that moving from "problem talk" to "solution talk" is a significant shift in the conversation. It is often useful to signal this move by asking something like: "Is it all right with you if I change tack slightly?" or "I've asked you a lot of questions about the problem. Could I ask you some different sorts of questions now?" With agreement from the interviewee, the worker can more easily shift the conversation toward a safety-oriented discussion.

Persistence is also important in using exception and other solution- and safety-focused questions. When training people in this approach we often emphasize the rule: Ask the question three times before you decide that there is no answer. Most interviewees expect workers to focus on the allegation/problem rather than discuss how to build safety. Therefore, persistence is often needed to reorient the conversation.

By initiating a conversation that elicits and illustrates exceptions, workers can demonstrate that they are interested in family members and believe there are times when they act capably. This sort of conversation can be invaluable in building cooperation and partnership. Family members begin to see that the worker wishes to work alongside them rather than disempower them. They learn that the agency will pay attention to their strengths and abilities and not simply adopt a narrow focus on harm and the abusive incident.

3. FAMILY STRENGTHS AND RESOURCES

The investigation of child abuse allegations can paint a very bleak picture. Michael White (1988) coined the term "problem saturated description" to refer to circumstances where the seeming enormity of the problem floods or saturates everyone's view of the situation, leading to feelings of hopelessness and impotence and preventing those involved from envisioning a solution. This happens frequently in child protection. It is therefore important to attempt to expand this picture. One of the easiest ways of doing this is to explore positive aspects and strengths of the family as identified by its members or acknowledged by other people or agencies.

This should not be seen as an attempt to minimize the abuse. Rather, it can reinforce the idea that the family's life and experience form a foundation on which change can be built. Berg (1994) considers the search for and acknowledging of family strengths one of the most productive and least exhausting ways for the worker to proceed.

Two case examples

A worker was given a long-term case in which the statutory agency had removed and adopted out four of the mother's children. The women suffered from mental illness and had neglected her children, though she still retained the care of a three-year-old girl. The statutory agency had grave concerns regarding this last child. The worker, who was new to the case, was told that no previous worker had been able to get through to this woman. Every one had given up on the mother. Visiting the mother in her home, the new worker allowed the conversation to take a very open-ended course while she watched the woman managing her child. In this way, the worker discovered that the woman wrote poetry, an activity that she found essential to her survival. Toward the end of the first visit that worker told the mother, "You know, others told me you couldn't cope, but

I see you coping; you write poetry to help keep yourself going, and, as I watch you with your young daughter, it's obvious that you really care for her."

In subsequent visits the woman showed the worker some of her poetry. The worker found the poetry very moving and let the mother know that she felt privileged to read it. She also continually highlighted times when the mother was appropriate with her daughter. In the same way, the worker also went on to elicit and highlight other strategies the mother used to cope with her situation, giving her time to talk about her sense of grief at losing the other four children. The two developed a strong relationship, and the mother's parenting, though never perfect, steadily improved. When asked how she managed to find out about these aspects of the woman's life, the worker answered that she simply believed these things were there all along.

The previous case demonstrates that the attitude the worker takes toward the family determines his or her ability to see a family's strengths and resourcefulness. Below is another example of how the worker's attitude can be instrumental in developing an understanding of the family's situation.

A teenage boy was behaving badly in his family, and the frustrated stepfather had begun to be violent in physically punishing him. As a result, the boy ran away from home. The statutory agency returned the boy to his parents, and the worker got the couple to come into the office. She proceeded to "read the riot act" to the stepfather, criticizing him for hitting the boy. In response, he walked out on the interview, submissively followed by the mother. The worker wrote up an assessment describing the father as overbearing and dominating of both mother and son. All this was seen to be occurring in a situation of escalating physical violence. The report also described a perceived lack of protectiveness on the part of the mother and denial on the part of the stepfather. It was recommended that the teenager be removed from home.

Another worker was assigned the task of following up with the family, and this worker decided to approach the family with an open mind, wondering whether her colleague's intervention had made a difference. Talking first to the mother alone, the worker discovered that the situation between the boy and his stepfather had improved considerably. The worker's description of what happened at this interview is as follows:

It was interesting because when I was given the information from the worker who originally interviewed them it was, "Get that kid out of that home, it's just a terrible place for him to be and the mother's not able to stand up to the stepfather." Yet in actual fact, she really was. She told me, "I've talked to my husband and I've told him he's not allowed to hit my son anymore, so there's no more hitting going on in this house." And I believed her because obviously that's what had made the difference. He'd started responding to the kid in a different way and the kid was now reacting to that in a positive way. So she actually did have quite a bit of power in that situation, it's just that he was so overwhelming in response to the confrontation at the office that that sort of information got lost.

The son confirmed the improvements reported by the mother. When the stepfather came home, the worker was quick to highlight to the man that things had improved and that he had clearly made a considerable effort. Two weeks later, following further reports of continued progress, the worker closed the case.

O'Neil and McCashen (1991), using what they call a competency-based approach, which involves acknowledging family strengths, have found that families reported that this focus made them feel that the worker was seeing them more holistically. It also demonstrated to the family that the worker had faith in their abilities to work through and resolve conflict.

Typical family resources and strengths that can be significant include:

- Extended family members who are willing and able to get involved and help out.
- Any relationships, whether with professionals or friends, that help family members feel good about themselves.
- A mother who finds the strength to stop associating with friends and family members with whom she has shared a lifestyle based on excessive drinking.
- A business partner of a man faced with charges of indecent dealings who tells his partner that he does not in any way condone sexual abuse of children, but that he will stick by his partner while he is getting help to change his behavior.
- A man living in a rural community who is open about his conviction of sexual molestation and finds that the members of the community do not alienate him.

- A maternal grandmother who tells her daughter, "You and I have been through so much, we are not going to let this beat us. Whether John (daughter's husband) abused Kylie (granddaughter) or not, we have to do everything we can to face the seriousness of this and make sure she is safe."
- A parent who has the courage to admit not only that she is unhappy with her parenting, but that she hates the fact she has been unnecessarily hitting and intimidating her child.
- A father who admits to friends and family that he abused his daughter.
- A father who attends a domestic violence course even though he is uncomfortable about it.
- A depressed parent who makes the effort to get involved with other people in a local church and organizes herself sufficiently to move out of a shelter and find her own accommodation.
- Any parents who, despite years of involvement with welfare and child protective services, make themselves as open as they can to work with the latest worker.
- A depressed mother who does not like her daughter still makes efforts to care for her. This same woman displays a significant level of honesty in admitting she does not like her daughter.
- A mother who, though she didn't want to face the possibility that her daughter was being sexually abused, realized that it might be happening and, over several nights, tricked her partner into confessing. The next morning she coolly got the children to come into the bedroom and forced the abuser to admit to them what he had done and why he would be leaving.
- A father who, after his wife committed suicide, fights his wife's family for the custody of his son. The young boy had been removed from his care due to the wife's sister's allegation that the father had sexually molested the child.
- A father who, after coming out of prison, determinedly and calmly persists through an exhausting two-and-half-year process to regain the care of his four children/stepchildren who had been taken from his ex-wife—a drug-user and prostitute—while he was in prison.

Assessing Behavior to Be a Strength

Many of the strengths described above were not readily recognized by the worker(s) involved and had to be highlighted by others. In fact, sometimes the strength was actually seen as something negative.

For instance, in the case of the father who fought for two-and-half-years after leaving prison for the return of his children, workers assumed that the real intention was to influence the Australian Immigration Department, which was considering having him deported. The husband of the woman who had committed suicide was told that his attempts to regain the care of his son demonstrated he was "in denial."

This highlights a delicate and subtle issue for child protection professionals. The behavior of both these fathers was a commitment to their children. However, in both cases, their actions also could have been a "performance" to protect their own self-interest or get their own way. In the second chapter we talked of the need for workers to suspend their judgments until they have gathered sufficient detailed information. This applies equally to adjudging something to be negative as to assessing it to be a positive. Making a positive judgment too quickly can lead the worker toward professional dangerousness. On the other hand, premature negative judgments will alienate service recipients very quickly. However, in almost every situation, there are some strengths that can be promptly acknowledged without danger.

Once strengths and resources are recognized as such, it is a vital aspect of the signs of safety approach to highlight them and to compliment whoever can be reasonably held responsible. This serves many obvious purposes, including building the relationship between family and worker and focusing attention on the sort of behavior that the agency wishes to support. It also serves to build optimism for the worker and family members involved.

Information about family strengths and resources can be elicited with questions such as:

- We have been talking about some very serious matters. To give me a more balanced picture, can you tell me some of the things that you feel are good about this family?
- If you were describing yourself to others, what sorts of things would you say you are good at?
- What do you like about being a parent? What have you learned from the experience?
- Can you tell me what you like about your dad? What sorts of things do you like doing together?
- What do you like about your son? What would you say he's good at?

- How do you usually solve family problems? Who does what?
- What do you do to cope in times of stress?
- Who do you turn to for help in dealing with problems? How do they help you?
- Who could best support you in dealing with these problems? How could they help?
- What do you do to help yourself deal with the pressures of raising children?
- Clearly, things have been really difficult for you. How have you coped with these pressures? What's kept you going?
- How is it that, even though you are faced with all this, you have been determined to do the best you can for your children?
- Can you tell me about the times when you get on well with your partner/child? What do you like about those times?
- What do you consider is good and what do you like about your family?
- What's good about your relationship with your child/mom/dad/ sibling?
- What do you think they would say is good about their relationship with you?

The answers to questions such as these, as with all responses to signs of safety questioning, provide information in two possible directions. Where a positive scenario about family life is generated, it provides insight into the constructive aspects of the family's relationships. Conversely, if family members can identify little or nothing that is positive about each other and their family, this may, in connection with other information, indicate that the problem is more severe than previously thought.

If the reader wishes to consider a strengths-based perspective, further useful material is contained in Weick, Rapp, Sullivan, and Kishardt (1989) and Saleeby (1992). Saleeby makes this very powerful and inspiring statement:

> At the very least, the strengths perspective obligates workers to understand that, however downtrodden or sick, individuals have survived (and in some cases thrived). They have taken steps, summoned up resources, and coped. We need to know what they have done, how they have done it, what they have learned from doing it, what resources (inner and outer) were available in their struggle to sur-

mount their troubles. People are always working on their situations, even if just deciding to be resigned to them; as helpers we must tap into that work, elucidate it, find and build on its possibilities. (pp. 171–172)

4. GOALS

The whole endeavor of child protection has one goal, and that is to create safety for children. We could not agree more with Weick et al. (1989, p. 353), when they write:

> In making assessment, both client and social worker seek to discover the individual and communal resources from which the client can draw in shaping an agenda. *The question is not what kind of life one has had but what kind of life one wants* and then bringing to bear all the personal and social resources available to accomplish this goal (emphasis added).

The foundation of the signs of safety approach is the explicit and careful focus given to the goals of both the family and the statutory agency. Very often in child protection work it is apparent what has to stop (the abuse or neglect) but the questions that remain unexplored are: How will it stop? What will happen instead? How will the agency and the family know? MacKinnon (1992) shows that service recipients consistently complain that they did not know what it was the statutory agency wanted of them.

It is essential that, throughout the case, the statutory agency clearly articulates—in concrete behavioral terms—what will indicate sufficient safety to close the case. Clear goals allow the evaluation of progress and help workers and family agree on when the case should be closed. While this is simple to say and compelling to believe, we know from experience that it is probably the most difficult aspect of the signs of safety model to implement. To achieve this, at minimum, requires detailed knowledge of the case and careful thinking on the part of the statutory agency.

It is also important to examine family members' views about how they would begin to create safety. For instance, a four-year-old child had been taken into custody, and the statutory workers had many concerns about the child's mother and her partner. They found themselves continually pressuring the family to take certain actions. The agency believed that the parents had not faced the realities of the situation that had caused the maltreatment. Therefore, they were also considering seizing the couple's recently born child. The previous case conference had resulted in a standoff between the agency and the parents, and the next one needed to be handled differently if a different outcome was desired.

The agency decided to begin the case conference by acknowledging that things hadn't been going well. Before any further discussion, the parents were asked to give *their understanding* of what the statutory agency required before they could return the child. The worker, supervisor, and case conference chairperson were all surprised when the mother articulated a series of ideas that would readily satisfy the agency. A case plan based on these ideas was prepared, and both family and workers left the conference with a new sense of confidence and direction. Following the case conference, the stepfather showed the worker a written list of complaints and grievances with which he had intended to confront the agency. He had not felt the need to read the list at the meeting, since he was satisfied with the conference's outcomes.

In this instance, both the agency and family were able to come to an agreement about what needed to happen to create safety for the child. Shifting the focus from problems to safety avoided the confrontation that would have arisen had the agency focused on defining the exact nature of the abuse. Instead, it promoted a conversation about future safety. Not surprisingly, the parents were more willing to implement their own ideas about creating safety for the child than ideas generated by the agency.

Questions to elicit the family's safety goals could include:

- Okay, we both see the need to make your child safe. What I'm really interested in are the ideas you have for doing this.
- How can we help you make things better and make your child safer?
- What do you suppose you, your partner, the child, other family members can do to increase safety?
- Let's suppose we could do anything to make your child safer. What would that be?
- In your opinion, what would it take to make your child safer?
- When we ask your son what would make him feel safer, what do you think he will say?
- For our involvement with your family to be useful to you, what would need to happen? What would change in your family? What would change about your partner/your child?

- How have you solved these sorts of problems before? How did you know to do that? How were you able to do that? Could you do that again?
- On those times when you've been successful with this child/situation, what was happening?
- As a parent/child, what would you really like to learn about this situation?
- If you got exactly the sort of support you wanted to deal with these problems and resolve them, what would that support look like?
- It's really clear to me that you don't want us continually in your life. What do you think we need to see to close the case?

Exploring Safety without Complete Agreement about the Abuse/Neglect

Often, service recipients are not willing to change simply to satisfy society's (or the government's) standards, but will be motivated by their own goal of avoiding (what they see as) outside interference in their family or to prove something to people they perceive as being critical of them. These sorts of "indirect" motivations and goals are often very powerful mechanisms for harnessing the energies of parents under investigation of child abuse. However, in such circumstances, the worker must carefully consider whether the family goals overlap sufficiently with the agency's goals to increase the safety of the child.

Agreement cannot always be reached, even on small issues such as whether a problem, let alone abuse or neglect, exists. Some families will continue to deny problems and even defend their right to behave in ways that others perceive as harmful. When the family will not admit to any problem or maltreatment, it is possible to get to a safety scenario by a more indirect route with a question such as, "I guess you don't want the hospital (school, doctor, police) to keep asking us to come and visit you all the time. What do you think they would need to see you do (about the child or about your partner) so they wouldn't keep phoning us with their concerns?"

Case example

This kind of question was used successfully in a case of alleged neglect. A bartender reported that a toddler had been unnecessarily hit by his mother for urinating on the floor of the hotel bar. It was reported that the child's mother regularly frequented the hotel with the child in tow, and little positive interaction appeared between the two. An investigation was conducted, but the child's mother was notably irritated by the report and the worker's visit. The mother listened to the allegation, but gave only a grudging acknowledgment that the worker's concern was valid. Instead of focusing on the reported incident, the worker made a decision to work with what the woman wanted. The woman definitely wanted to continue to visit the hotel regularly. The worker invited her to think about how she could do that while providing adequate care for her child, thereby showing the community that she was caring for him. The worker underlined that this would prevent further reports and subsequent investigations.

At first the woman could not see how to accomplish this. She asserted that she would simply refrain from visiting the hotel altogether. When challenged that, given her lifestyle, this was a rather unrealistic plan, the woman conceded that it was not possible. After further discussion, the woman came up with her own, more realistic, solution. She remembered that a friend had, in the past, offered to care for her son. Taking advantage of this friend's offer would allow her to drink in the bar while the child received adequate care. By focusing on the appropriate level of care and safety for the toddler, the worker did not have to focus on the facts of the reported event and unacceptable behavior. Instead, they had a conversation wherein the woman conceded that the situation was not appropriate for her child. To conclude the conversation, the worker made it clear to the woman that she would continue to visit and check that the plan they had made together was working. She also indicated that stronger action would be necessary if the toddler was in the same situation again.

Child protection workers often face circumstances where parents will acknowledge the problem in a limited way and then defend their actions. If, for example, a parent is defending his or her right to hit their child, the worker might make headway by considering this as a means to an end rather than an absolute goal. Questions such as the following could be productive:

- What are you hoping to achieve when you hit the child?
- What would tell you that you had obtained the result you wanted when you hit the child?
- Is this something you want to continue to do or are there other ways you can get your child to respond?

- What do you think it teaches your child when you hit him?
- Are there other ways of teaching your child this?

These questions focus explicitly on goals rather than problems. The worker should not see this as minimizing the problem or colluding with the family; rather, these questions are another way of exploring the situation. Not only do they aid in gathering further information, but they also have the potential to generate new ideas for increasing safety for the child.

Utilizing General Goals

Family members will rarely view the problem or its solution in the same way as the agency and its workers. Whether there is agreement between the parties about the allegations/maltreatment or not, it is invaluable to gain a more general sense of what family members want in their lives.

A single mother, adamant that she has not neglected her two children, may be motivated to move to a "better area" and obtain furniture, a washing machine, and new clothing for her children. The agency may assist her in these matters, from the perspective that if the mother achieves these things, she is very likely to have more energy for her children and also create a better environment for them.

On the other hand, a gregarious and friendly intellectually handi-capped woman had made it very clear to many workers over many years that she wasn't concerned about the problems that worried the agency, and she wasn't interested in being the responsible mother the workers wanted her to be. She was interested, however, in living a lifestyle that allowed her to go out regularly and "have a good time" with different men who were interested in her. The agency, which was continually and unsuccessfully trying to get the woman to be a responsible mother, finally got the situation unstuck when they began to take her general life goals seriously. Rather than insisting that the woman become responsible, the agency pursued other avenues to provide adequate, ongoing care for the children.

The worker who broadens his/her focus beyond the maltreatment issue, and even beyond safety, and shows a genuine interest in the family's aspirations for their life, both immediate and longer term, stands a good chance of creating another territory in which a strong connection can be built. Most people, not surprisingly, are respon-sive to the worker who shows a genuine interest in what they want to achieve.

Creating or Finding Overlap between
Agency and Family Goals

The challenge for the child protection worker when working with goals, whether general or specifically safety-focused, is threefold:

- Elicit the family's goals even if the family seems to be minimizing or denying the problems;
- Concretize the goals as being expressed by the presence of specific, measurable, observable, and positive behaviors; and
- Establish the extent to which these goals overlap with what the agency assesses as providing "protection and safety" for the child.

There will certainly be times when the agency cannot give the family everything it wants, but workers will never know what is possible unless they undertake a careful exploration of family's goals.

Here are some case scenarios that came about through focusing on family goals:

- A mother had been engaging in excessive use of drugs and physical self-abuse. The statutory agency wanted to remove the toddler from the mother's care. The mother did not want this. She insisted that she just needed a break and time away from her child. On this basis, regular day care was organized while the agency monitored the situation closely to see if sufficient improvement in the care of the child eventuated.
- A woman who described herself as an ex-addict came to a treatment agency and stated that she wanted her adopted children to be returned to her. The worker took her seriously and, in a step-by-step process of cooperation and assessing the mother's capacities, assisted the mother to pursue the options available to her.
- A homeless mother came to a child protection agency in chaos. She talked at length about her hopelessness, the total mess her life was in, and her despair over dragging her children through this. The worker asked the simple question, "Do you want your children?" This stopped the woman dead in her tracks and, after a pregnant silence that seemed to focus the woman, she replied that of course she did. The discussion then took on much more purpose and direction, and together they were able to take steps toward improving matters.
- A statutory agency investigated a situation where a preschool child

had ingested illegal drugs. Little progress was made regarding the allegation, but the mother made it clear she wanted to get a job, find independent accommodation, and leave her addicted boyfriend. The agency assisted her with these goals and the child became evidently happier and safer.

Case example

While at some point the agency's goals must be clarified and articulated to the family, the agency will often need to negotiate its goals with the family first. The case of the immigrant mother mentioned on page 57 is an excellent example of this.

Once the worker had developed cooperation and trust between himself and the mother, he was able to begin negotiating with her. The agency had an application for custody pending that would be dealt with by the courts. It became apparent to the worker that the mother believed that she would simply go into the court, tell the judge that she loved her daughter and wanted her returned to her care, and this would resolve the matter. The worker was able to explain that, in fact, the agency would call many witnesses, including her ex-husband, the psychiatrist she had seen, shelter staff, and friends to testify to the problems in her parenting. The reality of the situation became more evident to the mother. At the same time, the worker and agency were mindful that this court process was likely to devastate the woman, setting her in conflict or escalating existing conflict with almost everyone in her network. This was of particular concern, since she was already isolated enough as a recent immigrant, and such action would likely throw the woman back into acting out the worst aspects of her personality.

While listing her concerns about the child's father, the mother would make complaints regarding his irresponsibility. For example, when he would bring the child for supervised visitation, he would not provide spare clothes or diapers. Rather than dismiss these sorts of concerns, the worker took the woman seriously and pointed the problems out to the father, who, in turn, acted upon them. In this very simple yet concrete way the worker showed the woman he would take her seriously. With the case at the crossroads, the worker offered the parents a compromise. If the mother would withdraw her action to seek sole custody of the child, the statutory agency would withdraw its own court application and support both parents in continuing with the present arrangement, in which the father was the primary caregiver and the mother had regular access. The agency would continue to be involved to monitor progress. Both parents agreed to these arrangements.

It is a fundamental tenet of the signs of safety approach that substantive case plans should not be formulated until:

- The agency has carefully and explicitly articulated the safety goals it requires to enable it to close the case.
- The family and extended networks have been extensively and appropriately consulted regarding their ideas to resolve the problems and create safety and also their more general aspirations and goals.

5. SCALING SAFETY AND PROGRESS

Information gathered in child protection casework should be as specific and detailed as possible. Scaling questions can offer invaluable assistance in this regard. In the course of the investigation and casework, it is useful to routinely ask family members questions such as, "On a scale from 0 to 10—where 10 would mean things in this family are just the way you want them, and 0, that life could not be worse—where would you rate your family right now?" A question more specifically focused on safety could be asked in the following manner: "where 10 means that you are certain this sort of incident won't happen again and your son is safe, and 0 means that you think there is every likelihood this will happen again, how would you rate the situation at the moment?"

Scaling questions are of enormous benefit to child protection workers, since they create dialogue that automatically assumes a *continuum* from danger to safety. As any experienced child protection worker will readily acknowledge, a guarantee of absolute safety is never possible. Casework with families is carried out somewhere in the space between complete danger and total safety. By utilizing this danger-safety continuum, scaling questions, by the nature of their construction, embrace the possibility of change.

The signs of safety approach seeks to make child protection practice responsive and sensitive to family member's knowledge. Scaling questions are a very direct and straightforward way of accessing the perspective of the service recipient.

Case example

The case of the teenage boy who had been severely beaten by his stepfather (presented on p. 62) offers a good example. The worker asked the teenager to compare how things were four weeks previously, when he had been hit and had run away, with the present using a 0–10 scale (0, the worst things could be, 10, the best things could be). The boy stated that, at the time he made the complaint, things were at a 3, whereas the present score was 6. The worker then asked him what had made things better. The teenager indicated that "my stepfather is treating me a lot better now, he's letting me go out, he's still strict but he's listening to me and he hasn't hit me again." The worker described that:

> I then asked the boy, "Now that you're at a six what could make things a bit better?" and it was interesting the answer he gave me. He said that "it would be better if I was getting on better at school, then my life would be a lot better." This was entirely different from (talking about) any conflict that was going on at home, which made me feel reassured that in actual fact what the mother and the kid were saying, that things are better, was actually true.

Part of the value of scaling questions is that almost anyone can understand them and so, for example, they work very well with children. Their power also lies in the fact that scaling questions call for a very precise assessment from the service recipient, and this effectively turns the paternalistic paradigm of "the professional is always right," on its head. Since they privilege what the service recipient has to say, it is not surprising that scaling questions often evoke very significant information.

Working with Children

Due to the simplicity of scaling questions and because they frequently bring the dialogue straight to the point, child protection workers that we have trained readily utilize them in their interviews. Many workers have found scaling questions to be particularly useful in working with children.

Case example

In the following transcript a child protection worker* describes how she made use of scaling questions with two young girls:

---

*Kay Benham

WORKER   I went out on a joint interview with someone from the adoption branch. It was a stepfather who wanted to adopt these two kids, and through the adoption assessment a number of abuse issues had become apparent. The worker who had interviewed the kids about whether they wanted to be adopted or not was worried because they said, "No, we don't want to be adopted." And so the adoption worker decided, "Hey, this isn't part of my job," because she didn't know what she was getting into and so she referred it to child protection.

It was left to us to deal with the child protection issues—physical and sexual abuse. By the time we interviewed the kids a second time, it was really obvious to us that they'd been coached by the stepdad. They were painting this happy picture and how ideal life was and all the rest of it.

We were really getting nowhere with "Where would you rather be?" and "What's good about this family and what's not good?" It was "We don't care where we live" and "Everything's fine where we are" and a lot of "don't knows" and "can't remembers." So I decided to use scaling questions where things were really bad at 0 to the best they've ever been at 10, to find out where they would rather be. We used that question when they were with just with Mom, as opposed to when their stepdad had come onto the scene. And the difference was quite dramatic. We were able to expand on that in useful ways. And really it was obvious in using those questions that the family they were living in now was really problematic and really pretty awful.

ANDREW   So what brought out that information through the scaling questions?

WORKER   It was talking with the younger one really; the older one could maintain what she had been told to say. But the little one, I had a hunch it'd be best to go with her and so we got a number from her first.

ANDREW   What was her number with the stepfather then?

WORKER   With the one where she was now? About 3. And with her mom on her own was about 8. From there she (the youngest) was able to talk about what was better when Mom was there and what had happened since the stepdad had got there. So we didn't actually get a disclosure and I'm not sure anyway that abuse had actually happened—I think he was actually grooming her. I think it's part of that cycle.

But what was also useful about all of that was that we talked to the mom afterwards on her own and mom was able to make some connections with what the kids had said around the numbers. Then she started to talk about her own abuse. She said, "Well, I tried to tell my mom but she never listened." So it was really significant. She started to see that the same things that had happened to her were similarly happening to her kids.

Mom was shocked by how bad it was for the kids. I mean she really loves her kids, there's no doubt about that. She's very committed to them. We were really able to compliment her on that, and I was really aware of doing that much more to get her on our side. And we reinforced that she wanted to be protective and that she could see some of the parallels between her own experience and what was happening to her kids.

Some professionals become quite concerned when they begin to understand that the signs of safety approach invites children to give their own assessment of a situation. They seem to think that the model is therefore advocating that the worker takes whatever the child says at face value. This is not the case at all. The worker in this case was very relieved that the scaling questions elicited the children's own concerns and perspectives about living in a family with the stepfather. However, if the children had rated the latest living arrangement as equivalent to living with only their mother, the worker still would have been concerned (in fact, probably even more concerned). This underscores the fact that questioning family members simply provides *information* regarding their perspective. After hearing and processing the information, the worker and agency must make their own judgments as to what the answers mean in terms of risk and safety.

The child protection worker should not fall into the trap of thinking that a scaling question will necessarily generate positive information. In a case we will look at in more detail in chapter 5, the parents expressed complete disinterest in answering questions regarding their desire to have their children in their care. In another case involving neglect and some physical violence, the mother who seemed highly depressed, contended that on a scale of 0 (bad) to 10 (good) her life was presently at a 4. When asked to discuss the good things in her life that brought her up to 4, the woman broke down, confessing that her life was really at a 0. For the first time, the worker was provided with the opportunity to begin an honest conversation about just how bad things were in the woman's life. Therefore, it is important that the worker be open-minded about the sort of answers and information the questions will generate and not feel the questions have failed if something positive is not described.

Case example

Two children, an 11-year-old girl and her eight-year-old brother, had been taken into custody following allegations of sexual abuse involving their stepfather. Interviewing the 11-year-old on her own, the worker* asked the girl for her assessment of life in her family on a scale of 0 to 10. The girl responded, "Things are 0 and 10." In other words, at both ends of the scale. At the time, the worker could not make sense of the girl's response and thought perhaps that she was being evasive because she wanted to convince the worker that the situation was good enough for her to return home. Following the interview, the worker read through the transcript of the conversation and realized that, in fact, the girl was trying to tell her something important.

In a follow-up meeting with both children, the worker asked them to read a transcript of the interview, particularly drawing their attention to the answers they had given to the scaling questions. The worker told the girl she was unsure what was meant by the "0 and 10" answer. The girl readily clarified the worker's confusion. She described times when things were at a 0 (for example, those times when she was alone with her stepfather), and other times that were a 10 (when she felt safe and good about the situation). At this interview, the worker was delighted to find that the children effectively interviewed each other about their respective ratings and experiences in the family. This discussion provided information that had the complete integrity of the children's spontaneity.

Some workers have come to the conclusion that scaling questions are the signs of safety model in a nutshell. There are unlimited

---

*Kay Benham

ways in which the worker can utilize safety, progress, and similar scales. Further examples are presented in later chapters. One child welfare agency we are familiar with has undertaken the considerable task of creatively exploring and broadening the ways that scaling questions are used in child protection practice, utilizing not just numeric scales but also action methods, different graphs, and indicators (Deal & Veeken, 1996). The reader who wishes to become more familiar with the use of scaling questions should take the time to read some of the literature from solution-focused brief therapy, the model from which these questions have their origin (see, for example, Berg, 1994; Berg & de Shazer, 1993; DeJong & Berg, 1998; Hopwood & de Shazer, 1994; Turnell & Hopwood, 1994a & b).

6. WILLINGNESS, CONFIDENCE, AND CAPACITY

Statutory agencies often prepare child protection case plans that family members are unwilling or unable to implement. Child protection casework that incorporates a signs of safety approach should generate plans that families can act on. Ideas for action should be derived from solutions that that families have used before or should make sense to them, because they incorporate their position on the problem and reflect their own goals. Regardless of how ideas are generated, it is critical that the caseworker canvass the willingness, capacity, and confidence of family members.

The willingness, capacity, and confidence of service recipients regarding any plans for action are indicators of safety or danger. A parent might be willing to undertake a certain course of action and be confident it will make a difference, but have no capacity to undertake the plan because of a lack of resources or support. Sometimes one family member will lack the capacity to implement a certain plan because he or she feels that taking action will lead to negative consequences. For example, a child may know that talking about being abused might improve his or her safety, but feel unable to do so because of threats from the perpetrator or because of the fear that such action will split his family. A woman may know she can protect a child by taking herself and her children to a shelter, but feel unable to do so due to the fear of reprisals from her husband or disapproval from her extended family. Conversely, a family member may have the capacity to implement a certain plan (for example,

attend parenting classes or therapy, participate in a domestic violence group or a treatment program for perpetrators of sexual abuse),
but have little willingness to do so and no confidence that such
action will make any difference.

Child protection work often crosses culture and class lines. Just
because a young, white, middle-class social worker believes his or
her plan will bring about positive results does not in any way mean
that the members of a poor black family will concur. A careful
exploration of service recipients' perspectives regarding willingness,
confidence, and capacity is not only a good way of broadening the
danger/safety assessment but also an essential part of insuring that
the plans that are formulated will actually be implemented.

The following are questions related to each aspect:

Willingness

- On a scale of 0 to 10, where 10 means you are willing to do
  anything to make the child safer (stop the abuse) and 0 means
  you're not willing to do anything, where would you place yourself
  on that scale?
- If I (the worker) were to ask you to do _____, on a scale of 0
  to 10, how willing would you be?
- You talked earlier about the possibility of you doing _____. On
  a scale of 0 to 10, how willing are you to try that?
- What, if anything, would increase your willingness to do something about these problems?

Capacity to Take Action

- On a scale of 0 to 10, how would you rate your ability to do
  something about these problems?
- What aspects of these problems do you feel most able to tackle?
- On a scale of 0 to 10, how would you rate your ability to implement
  the plans we have talked about?
- What parts of these plans would you feel most able to try?
- What or who could help you do these things?
- How much control or influence do you think you have over this
  situation?
- I can see that you really want things to change, and you're willing
  to do almost anything to make that happen. To what extent do
  you think you can do something that will make a difference?

Confidence

- On a scale of 0 to 10, where 10 means that you are certain things will improve in your family and 0 indicates you think things will never get better, how would you rate things? What gives you that level of confidence?
- On a scale of 0 to 10, how confident are you that you (your family) can do things to make your child safer (stop the abuse)? What would increase your confidence?
- On a scale of 0 to 10 how confident are you that the perpetrator can change his or her behavior to make your child safer (stop the abuse)? What makes you this confident?
- Thinking specifically about doing _____. On a scale of 0 to 10 how confident are you that this would improve things?

Case example

The following case offers a good example of a worker creatively using scaling questions and exploring the issue of confidence with an intake allegation.

A worried grandmother phoned the child protection agency to make an allegation, expressing her concern regarding neglect and possible abuse of her granddaughter. The girl's mother (the daughter of the caller) was described as a drug addict with a predatory partner. When asked to rate the situation—10 being the best possible care was being provided for the granddaughter and 0 meaning that she was completely uncared for—the grandmother scaled the level of care at 2. She went on, at length, to say that the problems were all caused by the mother's partner. The worker,* being bombarded with very negative descriptions, wanted to explore the possibilities for change in this family, so she asked the grandmother what she regarded as being the best scenario for the child. The grandmother stated that this would entail the child living with her temporarily, then returning to her home when her daughter was no longer on drugs. The worker then asked, "On a scale from 0 to 10, how confident are you that this best scenario could actually happen?" The grandmother replied, "About a 2." This surprised the worker who, because of the extreme negativity, had expected a rating of 0. The grandmother explained that the rating was as high as 2 because

---

*Vania Dapaz

her daughter did love and care about her own child and wanted to fix the situation.

Still somewhat puzzled, the worker creatively used confidence scaling questions to clarify matters. What happened next is described in the worker's own words:

> I asked the question, "How confident would you be of your best scenario becoming reality if Jack (mother's partner) wasn't in the picture?" It went to a 2 1/2. So although through the whole conversation she blamed this man for her daughter's situation, just completely removing him out of the picture only moved her confidence a half point. That was really surprising. Once I turned it around and asked her questions about why it had only moved a half, it sort of really hit her and she said, "No, he's a problem but he's not THE problem. You've got to help my daughter."

At this point, the focus was taken off Jack and the worker was able to talk further with the grandmother about how they could work together to help her daughter. This is a good example of tailoring the practice elements to the particular case.

Signs of Safety Information Leading to the Removal of Children

The signs of safety approach is not just about discovering constructive aspects of family functioning. Using the practice elements can generate information indicative of either safety or danger. To conclude this chapter we want to present a case in which the elements of the signs of safety model were carefully explored, and the resultant information clearly underlined the need to remove the children.

The two children in this case had been badly neglected, severely beaten, and given inappropriate punishments such as being forced to sleep in an animal enclosure. A worker with considerable experience in utilizing the signs of safety approach had carefully explored all of the practice elements with the parents, the two children, and others close to the family. Despite this, the worker could find no exceptions, no strengths, and no resources that meaningfully related to family life or parenting. The parents' position was that the 11-year-old girl was "a lazy little bitch" who deserved everything she got, and both expressed complete ambivalence toward the six-year-old boy. Both parents were very clear about their goals. They did not want the children; they wanted the statutory agency to take them. The primary concern and interest in their life was the breeding and raising of pedigree dogs. The children had nothing constructive to offer regarding their family in any of the interviews. They did not want to be with their parents. The worker found alternative permanent placement for both children. The fact that the worker had done everything she could to elicit constructive information regarding family functioning and had drawn a complete blank confirmed that permanently separating the children from their parents was the best and safest option.

We have offered many questions that relate to each practice element throughout this chapter, but these should not be seen as prescriptive or, even worse, as the "correct" questions to use. The best questions and dialogue arise when a worker tailors the model, its philosophy, practice elements, and techniques to the specific case.

In the next chapter we look more closely at how these elements can be utilized at the intake stage.

CHAPTER FOUR

Starting out Right: The Referral

Good child protection practice is "front end intensive." Careful, detailed, and thorough work in the intake, investigation, and early planning stages will often lead to good, well-informed decisions and allow cases to proceed more smoothly to resolution. Child protection professionals must be thorough and rigorous in their information gathering. The signs of safety approach is beneficial in that it helps to collect a balance of information about existing family safety, competencies, and goals. Gathering good, detailed information at the beginning of a child protection case is vital, but it must be complemented by a strong emphasis on building partnerships and collaboration, not only with the family, but also with other professionals, extended family, and friends. Building cooperation among all involved will place the burden of responsibility for the child's safety on the shoulders of a broad network of people.

Some child protection professionals say they don't have the time to do these things. In a busy child protection agency, it is not uncommon for the sheer volume of work to overwhelm a worker's capacity to be this thorough. However, the more thorough workers are at the beginning of a case, the less likely they are to make errors of judgment or practice and the faster the conclusion of the matter can be reached.

THE BEGINNING IS THE BEST PLACE TO
START LOOKING FOR SIGNS OF SAFETY

The child protection process always begins with the notification. The initial process of information gathering (from the notifier and others) prior to direct contact with the family is the "intake" process.

The intake process is sometimes devalued or taken for granted in statutory agencies. In Western Australia, during a 1996 review of practice, it was found that new workers, nonprofessional staff, and even students on placement were commonly assigned to do intake. The quality and consistency of the information that guides subsequent intervention and decisions about whether to investigate or not are directly affected by the ability of the person doing the intake. Recognizing that more emphasis needed to be placed on this aspect of casework, the agency upgraded its approach, bringing experienced staff back into the intake role.

The intake role is also important to the signs of safety approach for another reason: It is the easiest time for child protection workers to begin to use the approach. Most notifications occur on the telephone. Workers have reported that they are more comfortable trying the approach in the safety of the office than in the more pressured environment of the investigation. For example, one worker placed a list of the practice elements, with relevant questions relating to each element, on the wall in front of her desk. During an intake phone call, it was easy for her to use these prompts to gather a balance of information. Later she would review the intake information to generate questions that might be asked during subsequent investigative interviews. When a balance of information regarding both the allegations and existing safety is gathered before meeting the family, it is easier to discuss their competencies and aspirations during the interview stage.

USING THE PRACTICE ELEMENTS
AT INTAKE

The intake worker must be mindful of building and maintaining a cooperative relationship with the notifier. Treating the notifier as an automatic relay station of information is a mistake. This person not only is a rich source of information, but may also have a relationship with the family that can be invaluable in the future. Therefore, the intake officer should elicit the notifier's concerns, perspective on the problems, ideas for improving the situation, and what they expected to take place as a result of the notification. Zellman and Antler (1990) confirm the importance of this thinking. They found that notifiers held strong views as to how the cases they reported should be handled. We will look again at the practice elements as they relate to the intake process to explore this more fully.

Respecting the Referrer's Story and Position

Obtaining the complainant's story is an important element in the intake procedure. The allegations need to be listened to and documented in detail both for the agency's needs and so that complainants feels that they have been heard. Paying attention to and being respectful of the notifier's position regarding the allegation is central to building cooperation. It provides an opportunity for gathering information about the case and learning whether a notifier has intentions other than the safety of the child. In general, callers want to be helpful and describe the problem as best they can.

Clearly, it is important to obtain as much detailed information as possible regarding the allegation. This will usually include: *who* (those involved and those who know about the problems), *what* (what they/others have seen and heard), *where* (where this happens), *when* (timeframe and the most recent events), and *how* the alleged abuse or neglect occurred. The distinction between events and judgments becomes important at this point. The position of the caller can be gleaned from a summation of the judgments s/he is making about the case. Child protection workers will be able to make better judgments about the case if they have a good understanding of the notifier's position.

The following types of questions may elicit more information regarding the notifier's position:

- What, in your view, are the worst aspects of the behavior you are talking about?
- What convinced you to take action and call us now?
- How is this behavior a problem for you?
- Have you done anything (apart from making the notification) to address the problem?
- What do you see as the cause of the problem?

- Have you talked about these matters with anyone who knows the family? Would others agree with your perspective? What would they say?
- Would the parent(s) of the family agree with your assessment of the situation?

A caller may believe that the blame lies with a parent, or perhaps with the abuse of drugs. They may see the situation as hopeless, requiring immediate removal of the children. They may believe in the possibility of change and be willing to be involved further. The notifer may be minimizing the facts and only making contact because they are obliged to (either by protocols or mandatory reporting requirements). Whatever the notifier's position, it is likely that more will be known about the case when their motivation is elicited and understood.

Exceptions and Strengths

Notifiers will often think more carefully about the situation they are describing when asked to explore exceptions and family strengths. If they recognize that the child protection authorities are seeking to take a more balanced approach, it may also ease their guilt about "turning the family in."

In many instances, the notifier is likely to know about exceptions, so the following questions may be useful:

- It sounds like this has happened before. What have you seen the family do to sort this out?
- You mentioned that it is not always like this. Can you tell me what is happening when the situation is okay? What is different about those times?
- Are there times when the mother is attentive rather than neglectful? Can you tell me more about those times? What did the parent and child do instead? What do you think contributed to the parent's responding differently?
- You said the child always seems miserable and withdrawn. Are there any times when you have seen her come out of her shell? What is she like then?

Some examples of questions that might be addressed to the notifier to elicit strengths and resources:

- How do family members usually solve this problem? What have you seen them doing?
- Are there times when they call on other people to help solve problems? When do they do that? Who do they call on?
- Can you relate anything good about these parents?"
- What do you see as positive about the relationship between the parents and their children?
- Are there aspects of your relationship with the family that, in conjunction with our intervention, might help to influence them for the better?

A public health nurse was asked what she liked about a mother (who she had reported for neglect). She replied, "You know, no one has ever asked me that, but she comes to every appointment without fail, and she is careful to always take her medication." This seemed to indicate that the woman could attend to detail, at least in some circumstances. This information could have been pursued in many ways. In this case it led to a discussion with the nurse regarding the quality of her relationship with the mother. This indicated another resource for the mother (i.e., the nurse) and showed that she could be involved in a cooperative relationship with a professional. The nurse was asked what the mother valued most about their relationship. The nurse speculated that the mother appreciated talking and being listened to, particularly when she felt down and discouraged. It became apparent that the nurse would be willing and able to play a part in addressing the concern.

Goals

In the intake context, there are two sets of safety goals that should be explored: the goals of the notifier and the safety goals that the notifier attributes to the family members. Questioning the notifier about these issues gives the worker a clearer idea about how the caller will know when the situation is resolved and often provides information about the caller's appraisal of the seriousness of the situation. Discussing safety acknowledges this, but shifts the focus from problems to possible solutions, demonstrating to the caller that something will be done.

Safety goals can be elicited with questions such as:

- The situation sounds serious. What do you think should happen? How would that solve this problem?

- Calling this agency is a big step. In your opinion, what would it take to make the child(ren) safer?
- What do you imagine us doing to make the child(ren) safer?
- Do you think any another agency might be able to help with this situation?
- What do you think this family should do? What are they capable of doing?
- I hear you saying that things are not right with this family. To give me a different view of the situation, can you tell me how you will know when the problem is solved?
- If this problem is solved, what difference will that make to you? How will your life be different?
- Are the parents concerned about these problems? How do you think the parents would go about resolving this?
- What do the children say that they want, or what do you think they want?

A dialogue regarding goals can also be initiated through the use of scaling questions. It may be appropriate to invite the notifier to rate the seriousness of the situation through a safety scaling question. For example, "On a scale of 0 to 10, where 0 means you are certain the child will be maltreated again and you believe we should act immediately and 10 means the problems are solved, where would you rate the seriousness of this case?" Following this question the worker can then inquire, "Given that you rate the situation at 3 (for example), what would you need to see to believe the situation had improved just enough to increase your score to a 4?" Using a scaling question in this way provides information about immediate progress rather than complete resolution.

Some callers contact statutory agencies with vague, nonspecific concerns, or concerns that reflect differences in parenting styles. For example, the caller might say, "They're neighbors of mine and I've heard the three-year-old screaming a lot. I think there might be some bruises on the kid's legs, but nothing really bad. They seem pretty rough with the kids. I feel sorry for those little kids," or, "They're always borrowing money/food and asking me to look after the kids. The other day they went to a ball game and left the kids with me all night after telling me they'd be back about 6 p.m."

Exploring what these sorts of callers want to see happen will frequently find them saying they want the statutory agency to make a single home visit and give the parents a "shake-up" or "scare them into being better parents."

Whatever the notifier's goals, the statutory agency needs to make its own assessment regarding action. As with all conversations about goals, the discussion serves to clarify whether the two parties are on a similar tack or not.

The questions associated with a signs of safety approach at intake are not necessarily those that the notifier would expect. It will often be necessary for the worker to explain the questions, perhaps ask for a little more of the caller's time, and acknowledge that the questions might be unexpected. In this way, the worker can be respectful of the caller and build cooperation. In some situations, notifiers will not want to participate in a discussion about what should be done because they believe "that's the job of the child protection services" and they've done their part by making the notification. In other situations, the caller will readily engage in a dialogue about safety, and this may indicate a willingness to be involved in improving the situation.

Child protection workers who utilize the signs of safety approach at intake tell us that they like the fact that the questions frequently make the caller think critically about the situation instead of simply dumping the case in the lap of the statutory agency. This applies equally to referrals from professionals as well as those from the general public. Given the trend in most child protection agencies throughout the world to teach the community that child protection issues are a collective responsibility, this sort of approach is also helpful in an educational sense.

Two cases of mostly self-motivated notifiers

The following is a child protection worker's* verbatim description of a notification by a grandmother regarding her own daughter's care of her grandchild. The allegations turned out to be motivated more by antagonism between the two adults than actual risk to the child.

> It was interesting to use the approach at intake. When I asked the grandmother whether there were any exceptions to the mother's household management and care of the children, she said, "No! No!

---

*June Bonar

No! None!" Then I asked about the mother's strengths. "She has none. The only strength she has is her domination. She dominates the family." It was just a stone wall, but that alerted me. I asked, "What would you like to see happen with this family?" and she thought and thought but couldn't provide any answers. Then I asked, "Well, would you like those things that your daughter is doing wrong in your eyes to be fixed?" She said, "Yes, I would." I thought that she seemed very opposed to the marriage. She thought her daughter should leave the marriage, and she was doing a pretty good job of undermining it.

This alerted me to the fact that I probably had a spurious complaint. She could see no good in her daughter and depicted the situation as very black-and-white. There was obviously some very strong animosity toward the mother. Even though I expected to see the house in a pickle (a mess), I felt that the grandmother was basically out to get the mother. So, the questions weren't wasted. They gave me an idea of the grandmother's motivation. It is easy to ask those questions. They are not out of the ordinary. Why shouldn't you ask someone with a complaint if there are any exceptions or times when the people you are talking about do cope? I didn't feel that those questions were strained. Her negativity alerted me to her real motivation.

In another situation, the notifier's self interest became evident when he was asked what would solve the problem as far as he was concerned. The allegation had been very general, related to neglect and possible physical abuse. The caller lived in an apartment next door to a single mother and her two young children. For this man, who worked third shift, the problem would be solved if the children were quiet from morning to midafternoon so that he could sleep.

Avoiding unnecessary confrontation

A child protection worker in a rural district office of Western Australia took an intake phone call from a schoolteacher regarding an eight-year-old Aboriginal boy. The child had been coming to school quite dirty, very late, often sleepy, and without any lunch. He had fallen asleep at his desk several days in a row and, on the day of the phone call, had come to school wearing pajamas that smelled of urine.

In Australia, the relationship between child protection agencies and the original inhabitants of the country are often strained, in part because Aboriginals were still being removed from their families simply because of their race well into the 1970s (Ralph, 1997). The family to which this boy belonged was not on good terms with the child protection agency, primarily because of the legacy of a number of the adults in the family having been raised in child welfare institutions. The worker was not looking forward to the prospect of knocking on the door of this particular family to discuss the allegation.

Though he had not yet made use of the signs of safety approach in which he had recently been trained, he thought this might be a good time to start. The worker decided to ask an exception question, inquiring of the teacher, "Are there any times when the boy is on time, attentive, and dressed appropriately?" The teacher immediately assured him that the boy was normally on time, involved in his work, and groomed reasonably, even if he was "a bit of a rascal." The teacher added that the boy was very popular and the fastest runner in his age group at the school.

The worker immediately had a new direction and new information to balance the concerns. He inquired if the teacher had any idea as to what might have precipitated this change? He had to ask the question several times, but eventually the teacher remembered that the boy's grandmother had died recently. Suddenly, things fell into place. It was very likely that many extended family members had come to mourn following the death and that the clan was focused almost totally on the loss of the matriarch. This may well have resulted in the boy's situation at school. The worker proposed to the teacher that they wait a week to see if things improved. The boy's presentation and behavior improved in the following week, and the home visit was not necessary.

While this is not a dramatic scenario of a severely at-risk child, it had considerable importance in the worker's office. The exception question, which the worker would not have asked in his usual practice, provided information that eliminated the need for a home visit. If the child protection worker had made a home visit at a time when the extended family was present and the clan was grieving, the situation could have become extremely difficult, if not explosive. The relationship between the statutory agency and the family in question (and, very likely, other Aboriginal families) would only have become further estranged.

The importance of cooperating with the notifier

A general practitioner of a town in a rural area phoned the statutory agency regarding a woman who had concerns about her 12-year-old nephew and eight-year-old niece. The woman had informed the doctor that, though she was not certain, it seemed that the 12-year-old boy was sexually interfering with the eight-year-old girl. The woman had been sick with worry and was not sleeping. After discussing the situation, the woman agreed that the doctor should consult with the statutory agency about what might be done. (It is important to note that, in the state in Australia where this occurred, there are no mandatory reporting requirements.) The doctor enjoyed a collaborative and mutually supportive relationship with the statutory welfare agency, was regularly involved in conducting medical assessments of abused children, and, in the past, had appropriately reported cases that required statutory attention.

The doctor phoned the child protection agency and received an aggressive response to the effect that she must disclose the name of the children involved or the name of the aunt. The phone call terminated, and the doctor was very dissatisfied. A few days later, the doctor and local child protection workers were in a signs of safety workshop being run by one of the authors. Discussion of this case in a small group exercise resulted in another standoff. The statutory workers again demanded the names and the doctor was on the defensive. At this stage, one of the authors (A.T.) became involved and offered to mediate by undertaking what amounted to an intake discussion on behalf of the agency. The local agency manager, who was concerned about the breakdown of a previously collaborative relationship, readily agreed with this proposition.

The author asked the doctor, "When you made that first phone contact, what would have constituted a successful call for you?" After a little thought, the doctor replied, "If I had been able to express my concern, confusion, and worry about the situation." Knowing that statutory agency workers are not employed simply to be a sympathetic ear for other people's worries, but also mindful that this might offer a path forward, the author asked, "Okay, so if your concern, confusion, and worry had been expressed and heard, what difference would that have made?" The doctor's immediately answered, "I would have been better able to help the woman (the aunt) take action." It was decided that the doctor would take several days to talk again with the aunt, encouraging her to make a notification. After this time, the doctor and a worker would talk again. Having reached this point, it was a simple matter to ask the agency manager if he was comfortable with the doctor proceeding along these lines and getting back to agency.

If the relationship between the doctor and the statutory agency had further deteriorated, not only would it have increased the risk to the eight-year-old girl in the question, but other local children would have become more vulnerable to maltreatment because of the breakdown in communication between key professionals in the child protection system.

It is easy to forget that the professional making the inquiry or referral is also a human being with his or her own concerns, worries, and hopes. Just as families want to feel heard and listened to, so do most referrers. It is important to deal with them respectfully and not simply treat them as a source of information.

An Intake Interview

To exemplify the use of the signs of safety approach, we have created, using actors, a case that we follow through the intake, assessment, investigation, and case planning stages. The transcript is based on a conglomerate of cases we have consulted on and is a typical scenario involving a young couple with a baby that has sustained injuries.

We begin with the intake interview. A doctor from a children's hospital notifies the child protection service about injuries to a baby.

DOCTOR My name is Dr. Peterson and I'm calling because there are some concerns about a child that we've admitted to the hospital.

OFFICER What are your concerns?

DOCTOR On examination, we found that the child has a greenstick fracture to the left arm and even more worrisome are two healed fractures in the ribs. We admitted the child today, and we're quite concerned about her.

OFFICER How old is the child?

DOCTOR Seven months old.

OFFICER And the names?

DOCTOR The baby is Jayne White; the mother is Mary Young.

OFFICER Have you talked to the parents?

DOCTOR Well, the baby was brought in today by the mother, who is a teenager. I've talked to her.

OFFICER Before I ask you about the mother, could you tell me more about the injuries?

DOCTOR Well, we would estimate the healed fractures to be in the vicinity of four to six weeks old.

OFFICER And the greenstick fracture, that's current?

DOCTOR I'd say that was within the last week.

OFFICER How did she come to the hospital in the first place, Doctor?

DOCTOR That's an interesting part of this story, I think. She had visited a local doctor with her aunt earlier in the week for the half-year check-up for Jayne, and the doctor noticed the baby's limp arm. He told her she needed to take the child to the hospital for an X-ray and it took her three days to get around to that. I'm not sure what that means exactly, perhaps only that she wasn't taking it too seriously, but that, of course, is a concern in itself.

OFFICER Right. And Mary, you said she's a teenager?

DOCTOR Yes, she's 18.

OFFICER Okay, how is she responding to all this?

DOCTOR She seems quite concerned about the child.

OFFICER How has she shown her concern?

DOCTOR She was upset about the injury to the baby and sad. She's a little confused. She never noticed that the baby was in pain, and although she's concerned, she doesn't seem to understand the seriousness of what we've uncovered. She says she has no understanding of how these injuries occurred. I've asked her what she thinks caused the injuries, but I got nowhere.

OFFICER What does she do when you ask her about the cause?

DOCTOR She avoids my questions altogether; she doesn't answer at all.

OFFICER I guess the other question is, what about a father?

DOCTOR I don't know too much. She says there is a father, his name's George. He's young too, and they live in a trailer park. I think she said he's at work, but I don't know any more than that.

OFFICER Okay.

OFFICER Do you know anything about their living circumstances?

DOCTOR She did say they had been living with her aunt until about two months ago. That interested me because the healed ribs would be less than two months old.

OFFICER Okay, what else have you observed about Mary?

DOCTOR Well, she wants me to know she really loves the baby, and that seems pretty genuine. The child certainly seems to have reached milestones, and the mother interacts with the child in the appropriate manner. But when I approach the subject of injury, she will not answer any of my questions. She doesn't seem to understand that a greenstick fracture and healed fractures in a child so young are of a very serious nature. We're talking about non-accidental injury here. That's very serious to me, and I think you need to get involved.

OFFICER Yes, we will certainly respond immediately. You said she is concerned about the child, and you also said that she responds appropriately to it. What have you seen that demonstrates this?

DOCTOR Well, she does appear to be concerned about the child's level of comfort. She's confident about changing and feeding. She's certainly doing all the right things there. At one point she was a bit abrupt and got impatient with the baby, though I'd be reluctant to put too much weight on that because this is fairly stressful for her. I'd say there's a reasonable bond between the two.

OFFICER What makes you say that?

DOCTOR The baby responded very well to her when she changed the diaper. When she brought out a bottle, the baby responded to her. The usual things you would expect to see with a baby that age.

OFFICER Like what?

DOCTOR Well, the baby allowed her to change the diaper readily, a bit of wriggling. She put a firm hand on the baby. There wasn't any undue pressure. When she picked up the baby to feed her, the baby sort of snuggled into her. It wasn't a mechanical feed situation.

OFFICER And you said the milestones are okay?

DOCTOR Yes, the child appears to have reached normal developmental milestones. There don't seem to be any other medical or developmental concerns here. The only concerns that I have at the moment are those injuries and their cause.

OFFICER So the baby was dressed okay, and clean?

DOCTOR Yes, the baby was dressed fine, the weight was fine, and, like I said, the milestones, the presentation of the baby apart from the injuries, are okay.

OFFICER Right, right. So it sounds like you've actually observed

Mary and had contact with her over some time this morning.

DOCTOR Yes, I spent a good two hours with her, on and off. I like the girl. She's very talkative about her child. She responds very well to compliments about her baby, but, like I said, the moment I want to move beyond that to these injuries, I get nowhere. I think you people need to come and do that now.

OFFICER And you've explained to her what our role is?

DOCTOR Well, I've explained to her that you're the Child Protection Services and under these circumstances, when a child presents at this hospital with what we call a non-accidental injury, then you must be involved. I'm not entirely sure she understood what I was saying.

OFFICER Is she cooperating with you in terms of the treatment of the child?

DOCTOR Oh yes, there's no question about that, so I think that I'd like to keep the child in the hospital at this stage.

OFFICER And is she willing to accept that? Does she know about that yet?

DOCTOR I asked her and she said that that would be okay.

OFFICER Obviously, that would be very useful to us in terms of undertaking an investigation and learning more about the situation.

DOCTOR We'd certainly like her to remain in the hospital as well.

OFFICER Okay. Have you got any sense of what the mother might want in terms of assistance?

DOCTOR I don't think she wants assistance of any sort. I think she just wants to go home with the baby.

OFFICER What do you want us to do now?

DOCTOR Well, I think you need to come down and talk to her. You're the people who do the investigations. We're going to keep the child here for 24 hours, but beyond that we'd like you to become involved and get to the bottom of how the injuries have been sustained. Until we know, I'm not sure she should have the baby.

OFFICER So, you feel that as long as she retains the position of avoiding the issue of injury, we might need to remove the child?

DOCTOR Yes, I think this is quite serious. This is a very young child, seven months old, with some serious injuries, and the injuries have escalated in a short period.

OFFICER It certainly seems that way. So, on a scale of 0 to 10, if the baby is left with the parents, how likely would you say it is that the baby's going to be that she is going to be abused, or suffer injuries again?

DOCTOR From what I see at the moment, I'd put it fairly high. I'd say about 8, if I had to put a number on it.

OFFICER So you'd be very certain that the baby would sustain further injuries if we didn't intervene?

DOCTOR Yes, particularly because there are so many unknowns at this stage. If the child remains in the hospital with its mother, I'd rate the risk very low.

OFFICER Yes, I think that's a benefit at the moment—if the hospital's willing to keep the child and the mother there for a little while, that gives us some space to move and act. Clearly, this is a serious case. I need to talk to my supervisor, but I'm sure we'll be coming down immediately. Are you on shift this afternoon?

DOCTOR I am, but I'll be difficult to contact.

OFFICER Would you be willing to introduce one of our workers to Mary? Would you be able to do that?

DOCTOR Yes.

OFFICER Okay. Is there anything more you think I need to know before I take this to my supervisor?

DOCTOR I don't think so. I think I've given you all that I can at this stage.

OFFICER Okay, thank you very much, Dr. Peterson.

The reader may be surprised that there are not more overt signs of safety questions in the dialogue just presented. There is no need for them, since the conversation with the doctor generated a good balance of detailed information regarding both danger and safety. This interview shouldn't be that different from interviews readers have participated in or would imagine themselves conducting.

However, it is worth noting the tenor of the interview. Following the example of this transcript, workers should remember to use their skills to engage people during intake. This means the referrer will be encouraged to talk more, and the interview will not conform to a forensic, "just-get-the-facts" format. This more engaging style will certainly lengthen the intake interview, but rarely by more than five or ten minutes. However, it frequently provides workers with more detailed information about the case and creates a context in which existing and future safety are more likely to be discussed.

The information we are seeking in the signs of safety process is often already available in existing cases. It is the way that the case is thought about and the information is utilized, assessed, and documented that make the difference. The signs of safety assessment process and its application to this particular case will be considered in the next chapter.

CHAPTER FIVE

Child Protection Assessment with Safety in Mind

Making judgments is inherent to child protection work. Decisions have to be made from the first moment information is taken about the case: Does this case warrant further investigation? Should it receive priority over others? Should two workers be involved in the investigation, or should the police be in attendance? Good judgments require detailed information.

Judgments in child protection cases are usually made on the basis of risk assessment methodologies, and, traditionally, risk assessment focuses primarily on issues of danger and harm. We believe assessment should also incorporate information about acceptable parenting, family competencies, strengths, and resources, and existing and envisioned safety. The signs of safety assessment process sets out to consider danger and safety simultaneously and to achieve a balanced, comprehensive assessment.

Risk assessment is integral to child protection activity and we want to comment on the benefits and limitations of traditional methods before we look at the signs of safety assessment process.

WHAT DOES TRADITIONAL RISK ASSESSMENT ACHIEVE?

Child protection practice can be extraordinarily difficult. Workers are always conscious that the well-being of children is directly affected by their assessments of risk. The use of formalized risk assessment systems has become an increasing trend in child protection in the 1990s (Doueck, Levine, & Bronson, 1993). Sound risk assess-

100

ment should be an automatic part of child protection practice. Built on the best research data available and integrated with practice wisdom, it should provide "thorough and consistent assessments" (Strathern, 1995, p. 5) regarding "the vulnerability of a child and a means of estimating the probable severity of any future instance of abuse or neglect" (Sigurdson & Reid, 1996, p. 3).

Initial casework (intake and investigation) in child protection usually revolves around gathering information about risk and harm. Information about such issues as the severity and pattern of the maltreatment, the perceptions of family members regarding abuse and neglect, the vulnerability of the child to future harm, the tendency toward violence within the family, and such additional factors as substance abuse, mental disorders, and any history of childhood abuse in the parents' lives, is typical of the data collected for the purposes of risk assessment (e.g., Sigurdson & Reid, 1996).

Most risk assessment maps are too one-sided: Focusing exclusive attention on the areas just mentioned is rather like mapping only the darkest valleys and gloomiest hollows of a particular territory. There can be no doubt that the child protection worker must gather information about past and potential harm and family deficiencies, but to balance the picture it is also vital to obtain information regarding past, existing, and potential safety, competencies, and strengths. This balance of information regarding family functioning allows the worker to achieve a comprehensive assessment of risk in child protection cases.

Risk assessment that becomes dominated by danger, harm, and the endless cataloging of risk factors often leads to a preoccupation or obsession with the problematic sides of family functioning, and workers become defensive in their case practice. This process is likely to limit the options for enhancing and building safety for the child.

Good risk assessment should provide a firm foundation for analysis, equipping workers with full and detailed information so that they feel secure in their ability to improve the child's situation.

Assessment Must Be Carried out with Cooperation and Change in Mind

An inquisitorial or "forensic" attitude can come to dominate child protection processes, and risk assessment focused primarily on harm and danger can accentuate this tendency. Where this attitude prevails, workers act as if their primary role is to gather the information required to complete the risk estimation task. The family may begin to feel alienated by the process when they sense that the information is being gathered simply to meet the needs of the professionals.

It is important to recognize that optimal information from the family will only be obtained in the context of the best possible relationship between worker and family. Practice informed by the goal of partnership will seek to use the gathering of information both to fulfill the requirements of risk assessment and to maximize the chances of building partnership with the family. Child protection must be carried out with cooperation and change in mind, and this must influence the manner in which information is gathered.

Assessment Does Not Equal Solutions

Traditionally, child protection risk assessment is designed to provide a clear appraisal of the nature of the abuse relative to the best professional knowledge of all abuse, thus providing a judgment about the severity of the particular situation and the likelihood of reabuse. However, this is no more than expertise regarding the problem. It does not necessarily mean a solution is any closer.

Change and safety in child protection is about the presence of something new, not just the absence of risk. Safety is far more substantial. In other words, the child protection worker not only needs to say, "stop doing a, b, and c" (factors relating to danger and harm), but also needs to be able to say, "do more of j, k, and l" (existing positive behaviors), and begin to do "x, y, and z" (new behaviors that will ensure safety).

The brief therapy tradition informs the signs of safety approach. The work of de Shazer and his colleagues teaches us that solutions aren't always as directly or linearly connected to the problem as professionals like to think. Certainly, the worker's solutions, developed from professional frameworks and logic, are often quite different from those of the family. When families are given a genuine chance to offer their own solutions through approaches such as signs of safety or family group conferencing, professionals are often surprised by the uniqueness of their ideas. Risk assessment systems and protocols should not constrain family or worker versatility in generating solutions.

Risk Estimation is Professional Knowledge, Not Family Knowledge

It is worth remembering that the whole endeavor of risk estimation is a professional way of understanding the vulnerability of the child within his/her family. This will probably differ from the family's perception of the situation, and the authority and expertise presented by professionals in the risk assessment process can easily overwhelm a focus on the family's voice.

Traditional risk assessment processes are built on professional wisdom and research-based knowledge. Therefore, workers may begin to privilege their professional knowledge as superior to family knowledge. If this occurs, the chances of cooperation, and thereby the likelihood of change in the family, will be reduced. Since partnership is essential to safety, and a clear understanding of the family's perspective is essential to partnership, traditional risk assessment processes can create their own risk for the child if they overwhelm or even subjugate the family's voice and perspective regarding the problems and solutions.

Professional risk assessment must be balanced by the systematic drawing-out and integration of the family's perspective. This is the balance that the signs of safety approach creates. Therefore, since partnership, cooperation, and change are the goals, there must be some careful bridging between family knowledge and professional knowledge.

One Australian statutory child protection agency, the Department for Human Services of Victoria, was aware of this dilemma when developing its own risk assessment framework. They took the unusual step of actually sitting down with a small group of child protection service recipients and presenting to them the risk assessment framework they were developing. The service users' perspective was instructive. They responded by saying they wished they had been aware of the framework when they were being investigated, as this would have helped them make sense of the judgments the workers were making about them.

BALANCING DANGER AND SAFETY: THE SIGNS OF SAFETY ASSESSMENT

Since the child protection endeavor operates on a continuum somewhere between absolute safety and complete danger, we head our assessment form with a two-headed arrow between the two ends of the continuum (see the blank form on p. 104). The heart of the signs of safety assessment process involves listing information indicative of both safety and danger. This process can be best demonstrated as we consider a postintake assessment in the case of Mary's baby (p. 105).

Signs of Safety Assessment and Planning Form

DANGER → **SAFETY**

(You may wish to spatially locate items between the danger and safety poles along this continuum.)

List all aspects that demonstrate likelihood of maltreatment (past, present, or future).

List all aspects that indicate safety (exceptions, strengths and resources, goals, willingness, etc.).

Safety and Context Scale

Safety Scale: Given the danger and safety information, rate the situation on a scale of 0-10, where 0 means recurrence of similar or worse abuse/neglect is certain and 10 means that there is sufficient safety for the child to close the case.

Context Scale: Rate this case on a scale of 0 – 10, where 10 means this is not a situation where any action would be taken and 0 means this is the worst case of child abuse/neglect that the agency has seen.

Agency Goals What will the agency need to see occur to be willing to close this case?

Family Goals What does the family want generally and regarding safety?

Immediate Progress What would indicate to the agency that some small progress had been made?

Mary, George, and Jayne; Post intake.

Signs of Safety Assessment and Planning Form

DANGER ⟵ ⟶ **SAFETY**

(You may wish to spatially locate items between the danger and safety poles along this continuum.)

List all aspects that demonstrate likelihood of maltreatment (past, present, or future).

1. Baby has fracture to left arm.
2. Baby has healed fractures on ribs; indicates history of injury.
3. Baby aged 7 months.
4. Mary says she doesn't know how injuries happened.
5. Mary becomes withdrawn when issue of fractures discussed.
6. Mary not aware of injury, discovered by local doctor.
7. Mary took 3 days to bring baby to hospital.
8. Mary seems ignorant of injury and its significance.
9. Mary and George both very young parents.

18. Live in a trailer park, may be isolated.

List all aspects that indicate safety (exceptions, strengths and resources, goals, willingness, etc.).

10. Injuries have come to light and baby's health is being monitored by hospital.
11. Mary is attentive and cares appropriately; responds to crying, changes and feeds baby regularly.
12. Dr describes reasonable bonding between Mary and baby.
13. Mary says she loves baby and it "cuddles into her".
14. Baby is clean.
15. Developmental milestones of baby O.K.
16. Mary wants to take baby home and willing to stay in hospital while baby cared for.
17. Mary willing to talk to statutory agency.

Safety and Context Scale

2 | **3**

Safety Scale: Given the danger and safety information, rate the situation on scale of 0–10, where 0 means recurrence of similar or worse abuse/neglect is certain and 10 means there is sufficient safety for the child to close the case.

Context Scale: Rate this case on a scale of 0–10 where 10 means this is not a situation where any action would be taken and 0 means this is the worst case of child abuse/neglect that the agency has seen.

Agency Goals
What will the agency need to see occur or to be willing to close this case?
i Knowledge of cause of injuries elicited and responsibility taken by perpetrator.
ii Safety plan in place to protect against any further injury.
iii Responsibility taken by parents to implement plan.
iv Implementation of safety plan demonstrated by parents over time.

Family Goals
What does the family want generally and regarding safety?

Mary's goals:
i Care for her child in own home.
ii Be a good mother.

Immediate Progress
What would indicate to the agency that some small progress had been made?
i Mary to understand significance of injuries.
ii Worker to build a positive relationship with Mary.
iii Discover Mary's explanation for injuries.
iv Arrange to meet with and interview George.
v Create immediate safety plan for Jayne.

The issue of the actual incidence of abuse or neglect always needs to be considered first. In this case, point 1 lists the baby's fracture to the left arm. Point 2 describes the healed rib fractures, which indicate a history of injury. Point 3 lists that the child is preverbal and under 12 months, which is a significant indicator of danger (Sabotta & Davies, 1992, for example, demonstrate that a baby less than one year old, with a pattern of injuries, is the classic child maltreatment scenario with considerable risk of homicide).

In all assessments there will be other aspects of the situation that contribute to potential danger. In this situation, it is of particular concern that the mother does not know how the injuries occurred (point 4), that she becomes withdrawn when the issue of the fractures is discussed or she is asked how they might have happened (5), that the mother was not directly attentive of the injury; it was picked up by the local doctor (6), and it took her a further three days to come to the hospital (7). This all seems to indicate ignorance of, or desire to avoid the seriousness of the problem (8). Finally, the fact that the parents are both teenagers is a standard child protection risk factor (9).

On the safety side of the equation, the most important sign of safety is probably the fact that the injuries have come to light and the baby's health is being monitored by the hospital (10). Additionally, the doctor has indicated that the mother is attentive toward the baby, responds to its crying, changes it, and feeds it appropriately (11), the doctor reports "reasonable bonding" between mother and baby (12), the mother says she loves the baby and it "cuddles in to her" (13), the baby is clean (14), developmental milestones check out okay (15), the mother wants to take the baby home but is willing to stay in the hospital while the baby receives medical attention (16), and the mother is willing to talk to the statutory agency (17).

These factors have been placed at either end of the continuum because they are more or less indicative of safety and danger, respectively. Other aspects are not always quite so clear. For example, the fact that Mary and George live in a trailer park may indicate that they are isolated and lacking in support. On the other hand, the park may be a friendly environment, with neighbors who could be helpful. So, balancing these considerations, we have placed this factor (18) toward the middle of the continuum, a little more on the danger side. Further information from subsequent interviews should clarify its significance and positioning.

Placing the facts on a continuum between danger and safety

immediately operationalizes the distinction we drew (in chapter 2) between the details of the case and the judgments attributed thereto. It is important to approach the danger-safety continuum as being merely representational. Worker judgment, not empirical weighting, supports the assessment. The process will also lose its dynamism if workers become obsessed or pedantic about where a particular detail should be placed on the continuum. This will bog the assessment down. Supervisors should be mindful of this when utilizing the approach with teams of workers. It is important to hear different perspectives, but not to allow these to degenerate into arguments. In any case, an overall assessment of the situation will be called for as the process unfolds.

Professionals will have their own perspective(s) regarding the different facts, but clients will also have their judgments on the matter. For example, the fact that the couple lives in a trailer may be seen as positive by the mother. She may be proud of it as the first home of her own, enjoy the fact that she is beside the beach, and get support from other trailer park residents. On the other hand, she may feel that the trailer is cramped, that people are nosey and critical, and that she has no space. At this stage, we don't know. The statutory agency might have other views about whether the trailer park is good or bad. The park may have a reputation for excessive use of alcohol and drugs as part of a beach culture, or it might be a quiet and safe environment. It might be isolated from services or close to them, and so on.

As we have noted, the facts and details of the case can get intertwined with judgments, and it is best for these to be teased apart. The more mindful workers are of the judgments they place on information, the more likely they are to clarify perceptions with the clients and remain open-minded while gathering information within the assessment process.

Safety and Context Scale

The safety and context scales draw the information into two summary judgments with 0 to 10 ratings. The safety scale concerns the particular case and asks for a rating where 0 indicates the child is certain to be abused again and 10 indicates that there is sufficient safety present for the statutory agency to close the case. In the case just presented, numerous child protection workers have considered the information and given it an average rating of 2.

The context scale considers a particular case relative to all the other cases that the statutory agency deals with and again asks for a rating on a 0 to 10 scale. This time, 0 is indicative of the worst case the statutory agency has ever been involved with, and a rating of 10 indicates a case in which the agency would take no action whatsoever. The purpose of this scale, as the title suggests, is to provide a context for the safety scale rating. For example, consider a case of a child being "disciplined" by his parents. The hitting does not leave any bruises, but it has occurred regularly, perhaps three to four times per year, for many years. The safety scale would need to be rated at a 1 or even 0, since it is almost guaranteed that the child will be hit again. However the context scale (assuming the child is well-loved, healthy, progressing well at school, and so on) would probably be 8, 9, or even 10 depending on the country in which the incident occurs. The case is likely to be closed fairly promptly.

Workers who considered the details in the case of Mary and Jayne proposed a context scale rating of about 3.

GOALS

A focus on goals lies at the heart of the signs of safety approach. As we have mentioned, consumer research tells us that clients are usually uncertain about what the statutory agency wants, and the client's goals are frequently unexplored by the agency. To address this problem, the signs of safety assessment process and worksheet call for the goals of the agency and the goals of the family to be considered even before the family has been met. In this way, the approach operationalizes the notion that if the worker starts forming a realistic idea of where the case needs to go from the outset, it is more likely that both the agency and the family will get there expeditiously.

Agency Goals

Some might consider it preemptive to ask the agency to define what it needs to see to close the case before it has seen the family, based only on intake information. However, many cases are closed following intake or after a single investigative interview. In the United Kingdom, 75% of all cases are finalized by this stage (Dartington Social Research Unit, 1995), so this practice correlates directly with what happens in actual casework. Furthermore, the goal in child protection activity is always to ensure enough ongoing and continuing safety for the child (preferably within the family) to close the case. Focusing on these ideals will allow more purposeful casework and contact with the family.

In the case of Mary's baby, achieving the following goals would enable the agency to close the file: (1) The perpetrator takes responsibility for the abuse and the details of the injury are brought to light. (2) A detailed safety plan is set in place to protect against any further injury. (3) The family takes responsibility for implementing the plan. (4) Implementation of the safety plan is demonstrated to the statutory agency over a reasonable period of time.

Family Goals

Naturally, parents have aspirations and goals for their children. Involvement of child protection professionals will usually threaten parents' goals for their children and interfere with their autonomy in raising them. Understanding parents' goals for their children, how they want to care for them, and how they are already doing this is a joining mechanism "par excellence" for the child protection worker. Quite simply, if parents feel that the worker understands and will listen to what they want, the process of partnership between parents and caseworker is well underway. This wards off the parents' sense of powerlessness and gives them the sense that they have important input into the direction of the case.

It appears that Mary wants to care for Jayne in her own home, and her active care for the child indicates that she wants to be a good mother. The reality of Mary's goals, relative to the safety sought by the agency, will be determined through the investigation and casework process that will follow.

Further details about what the parents want cannot be inferred from the intake discussion. However, it is not necessary to create ideas that aren't evident from the information. This process seeks to "start as we intend to continue" by orienting the professionals toward thinking about what the family wants. Any good assessment process should organize information as well as highlight gaps in available knowledge.

Immediate Progress

The signs of safety assessment and planning process asks the worker to consider not only the long-term goals of the agency and the family, but also what can and should be achieved in the immediate future. Workers should consider small things that could increase the agency's assessment of safety by a small increment, perhaps half a point or less. This is a simple way of attending to immediate goals. For example, in the case we are following, some workers would be aiming (explicitly or implicitly) to find out everything about how the injuries were sustained and to gain an admission of responsibility during the first investigative interview. While this would be a very satisfying result if it were achieved, it is more likely that the worker with these criteria for immediate success will be disappointed. This is not to say that this can't occur during the initial investigation. However, these sorts of large goals may result in the worker's becoming frustrated and, in the worst scenario, becoming aggressive and confrontational in contact with the clients.

We would suggest (particularly given that the child is safe, and under constant supervision for the time being) that the worker set him or herself smaller goals for the initial contact: (1) Mary should understand the significance of the injuries. (2) The worker will build a positive relationship with her. (3) Mary's explanation for the injuries will be discovered. (4) A subsequent interview will be organized with George. (5) A plan to ensure Jayne's safety in the immediate future will be created, and the parents will be involved in this as much as is possible.

These are small goals, but they will still be challenging for the worker. If they are achieved in the first interviews with Mary and George, the worker will have made significant progress.

CHAPTER SIX

Knocking on the Door: More than an Investigation

Gather a group of child protection workers anywhere in the world and ask them to describe the most difficult aspect of their role, and they will inevitably talk about interviewing parents for the first time in a new investigation*. No amount of training can fully equip workers to deal with the anxiety of knocking on a door to tell a complete stranger that they are under suspicion of maltreating their children.

At this stage, the pressure comes from every direction. Family members usually feel overwhelmed, defensive, angry, threatened, withdrawn, helpless, etc. Paradoxically, they also need the worker to help them understand what they are accused of, what might happen, what they can expect in the agency-family relationship, and what they can do. The statutory agency expects the worker to quickly gather and assess a lot of complex and intimate information about the family and to decide the extent to which the child(ren) have suffered or are at risk of harm. Workers must also manage their own doubts and fears: Have I got it right? Have I done enough? Have I placed the child at risk? Could what I have done result in an inquiry?

The biggest challenge to good practice at this point is for the worker to remain open-minded about the family and the parents.

---

*Terminology differs around the world, but, for the purposes of this book, the investigation is seen as the initial series of interviews that begins with the first contact between the worker and immediate members of the family to which the allegations refer.

111

The temptation to make definitive final judgments is considerable. The worker needs to squarely face the realities and ugliness of the alleged or actual maltreatment without dehumanizing or demonizing the parents. This requires a receptiveness and open-mindedness that allows for possibilities and change without minimizing the level of harm or danger.

The initial investigation has three purposes:

- Assess the truth of the allegations.
- Assess the likelihood of future harm.
- Build as much cooperation as possible so that the best information is gathered and a partnership between the family and agency is achievable should ongoing casework be required.

There is a tendency in the child protection field to reduce the investigation task to the first two purposes (the gathering of information to fulfill assessment and substantiation requirements) and overlook the relationship between the worker and family. This tendency is understandable, since it seems efficient and focused, but it will quickly become counterproductive. Without an emphasis on the worker-family relationship, the likelihood of antagonism between the parties increases, as does the corresponding likelihood of greater statutory intervention. A sole focus on the first two aims can easily slide the casework into Parton's "blaming system." Partnership-aspiring child protection work requires skillful practice that is simultaneously authoritative *and* open-minded.

A central theme of this chapter will be to explore the difficult task of bringing coercion and cooperation together, so that the initial contacts with the family result in more than just an investigation. Allegations need to be rigorously examined while the worker keeps the family positively engaged in the process.

CHARACTERISTICS OF A
WELL-HANDLED INVESTIGATION

In their analysis of 220 child protection cases, Thoburn et al. (1995) compared the difference between situations that were conflictual and those that were cooperative. They found the difference was partly the result of *"well-handled investigations,"* in which clients and worker formed an alliance in the crisis stage of contact. Even in the most difficult of cases, the key factors in fostering this sort of partnership were "the attitudes, skill and efforts of the social workers backed by agency policies and procedures" (p. 229).

A well-handled investigation should involve:

- An exploration of the allegation based on the usual agency protocol for examining danger and harm, incorporating full input from family members regarding their perspective on the allegations.
- Integrating into the examination of risk an exploration of signs of safety, including past and present protectiveness, family strengths and resources, and the family's own plans for increasing safety.
- Listening carefully to the family's experience and letting them know they have been understood.
- Sensitivity and empathy for the anxiety that the investigation will provoke within the family.
- A very clear and open stance concerning the agency's statutory role and authority.
- An up-front and honest attitude about the allegations.
- Conducting the interview slowly and flexibly.
- Focusing on small steps and making sure each step is understood, while recognizing that not everything has to be accomplished at once.
- Providing choice and the chance for family members to provide input wherever possible.
- Interviewing for information rather than solutions. Workers can take some of the pressure off themselves by working to gather the best possible information rather than trying to quickly arrive at decisions and plans. Finding solutions is best left for later in the casework process.

INTEGRATING THE SIGNS OF SAFETY
APPROACH INTO THE INVESTIGATION

When we began training child protection workers to use the signs of safety approach, we had a notion that the practice elements could be used in a fairly predictable structure commencing with the allegation, eliciting and understanding the position of the client regarding the abuse, considering the risks (using agency protocols), exploring exceptions, strengths, and the family's goals, and finally scaling willingness or motivation to take action.

Of course, we soon found that real life worker-family interactions rarely allow the approach to be followed in such a neat, linear fashion. There is no one right way to use the model or its strategies. The practice elements find best expression in the natural ebb and flow of a purposive conversation. Each situation is unique and therefore demands a unique response. Dean and Locke (1983) make their point well when they state,

> There are not any perfect phrases that a worker can learn, and an undue reliance on technique leads to sterile practice and depersonalization. Each worker should use his humanity to develop a personal style that allows congruence within self and in transaction with clients. (p. 98)

The signs of safety elements provide an increased repertoire for workers, which enhances the possibility of partnership. However, people should not be led into partnership solely through techniques. Partnership is about the worker and service recipients together constructing a collaboration unique to the situation. If the seeds of a partnership can be planted at investigation the likelihood of collaboration in subsequent casework will be dramatically improved.

Investigation Interview with Mary

To illustrate the use of the signs of safety approach, we continue to follow its application to the case of Mary's baby by looking at investigative interviews with Mary and with George.

DOCTOR   Hello, Mary. This is Jonathan Browning from Family and Children's Services. You remember I told you he'd be coming to meet with you?

MARY   Yes.

WORKER   Hello, Mary. Dr. Peterson has been telling me a bit about you and the baby. I hear you have a lovely baby.

MARY   Uh-huh.

WORKER   Dr. Peterson tells me you get on pretty well with her.

MARY   Yeah. Well, I'd rather be with her right now than stuck here, I can tell you.

WORKER   Of course.

The worker wants to build an immediate connection with Mary. Compliments are a good way to do this. As a consequence, the conversation had begun with a degree of positivity, and Mary's desire to be with the baby—an important sign of safety—is also reconfirmed.

> MARY But Dr. Peterson said I have to sit and talk to you.
>
> WORKER Do you know why I am here and what I do?
>
> MARY Are you the welfare?
>
> WORKER Yes, I am. I'm from Family and Children's Services. Some people call us "the welfare" because part of our job is to look after the welfare of children and families. We get called in when children have been hurt or look like they've been harmed in some way. It's our job to talk to the parents to figure out how it happened and sort out with the family what will help to make sure it won't happen again. Does that sound anything like what you've heard about the welfare?
>
> MARY Yeah. I s'pose you want to ask me questions about baby. Are you gonna take her away from me?
>
> WORKER Well, I want to talk to you about Jayne and the fracture to her arm. To be honest with you, I can't say what's going to happen until we have talked more, but we are very concerned about Jayne. We may ask you to let her to stay in the hospital until we understand how this happened to her and believe she is safe to go home.

At this point, the worker must be honest and succinct about the agency's involvement and authority. It is important that the worker not understate the agency's capacity to apprehend the child from the family. MacKinnon (1992) describes how parents can feel betrayed by a worker who starts out by acting like a friend and then suddenly, without warning, invokes statutory powers. Like many people investigated by child protection professionals, Mary asks, "Are you gonna take her away from me?" This gives the worker the opportunity to clearly describe his role without appearing authoritarian or apologetic.

It is a small but important point (good interviews are usually an incremental process of such small points) that the worker talks about working together with Mary to create a situation where the baby is safe to go home. His role is not confined to finding out what happened in the past, but includes setting the scene for a focus on safety in the present and future.

MARY   But she is safe with me. I wouldn't let anyone hurt her. Honest!

WORKER   Before we talk about the injuries, I'd like to tell you what Dr. Peterson has said about you and Jayne. It's pretty clear to the hospital that you work hard to look after Jayne. She's a clean and well-fed baby, and she certainly loves being with you and cuddling into you.

MARY   Yeah, and I do look after her. I do feed her well. Like I said to Dr. Peterson, I don't know a lot about babies, and I need to learn more about it. But I do know what she eats and when she needs to eat, how often and when she needs changing, and things like that.

WORKER   And that's very clear to us all, and it's also very honest of you to admit what you don't know. Were you expecting to have a baby?

MARY   No.

WORKER   Was it a shock when you first found out you were pregnant?

MARY   A shock to George, I tell you. It was sort of a shock to me too, but it's quite nice, really. I like it.

WORKER   George didn't think much of having a baby?

MARY   Well, he's a lot younger. He's a year younger than me. He was only sixteen when she was born.

WORKER   Oh boy. So does he feel like he's got to settle down now and be a dad and all that stuff?

MARY   Well, sort of (*pauses*), I mean, I don't know whether he will settle down. It's not the same for dads, you know. She doesn't cuddle into him like she does with me. Dr. Peterson said she was a bit annoyed that she hasn't seen George. I wondered why George didn't come in when he dropped me off.

WORKER   You're not sure?

MARY   No. I think he's got other things on his mind, work and things. He wants to do something different. I mean he can't go off and do his own thing. He had to get a job because we needed some money and we couldn't get a place or anything. He has to look after her, too.

WORKER   What's it like for you to know that he doesn't really like having the baby around?

MARY   You know, I can't understand anyone not wanting her.

WORKER She's so cute. I just like having and doing things for her. It's nice.

WORKER Does George do things like changing the diapers and such?

MARY He doesn't like changing the diapers. (*Both laugh.*) Sometimes he has to because I have to leave her with him when I go shopping. I don't like to take her shopping, especially when it's winter and it's cold and wet outside. I leave her with George, and sometimes I'm away for a couple of hours. He has to change the diapers and do things like that. He doesn't like it; he gets really annoyed with that. But he does it.

Dr. Peterson has indicated that Mary doesn't like talking about the injuries, and the worker decides it is important to build the relationship before moving to this subject. Using intake information about Mary's strengths and the responsible behavior that she has demonstrated as a mother provides useful material to this end. The direct compliments about her parenting lead into a discussion that reveals useful information about Mary and George, their life, and parenting styles. This is information that provides indications of both the safety and dangers in the family.

In this next section of dialogue, the worker returns overtly to the matter of the injuries, enhancing the possibility of cooperation by offering Mary some choice as he changes the subject.

WORKER Is it okay with you if we talk about the injuries now?

MARY If we have to.

WORKER Okay. What did Dr. Peterson say about how she thought it could have happened?

MARY She said babies get that sort of injury with a really hard pull, like if someone is changing a baby and is rough or maybe pulled her away from something, or pulled something away from her. She asked if I did that. I wouldn't do that. I wouldn't hurt her, not in a million years.

WORKER So you can't understand how anybody else would hurt her like that?

MARY No. No. Dr. Peterson seems to think that I did it. And I didn't. I didn't. Honestly. I don't know. Quite honestly, I think it happened when she was doing something in the cot or maybe on the floor. That could have happened, couldn't it?

WORKER   I don't think so. It's going to be hard, but we need to get to the bottom of this.

MARY   What's going to happen?

WORKER   That's a good question, and I need to be frank with you. At the moment, with the injury to the arm and old injuries to the ribs, we cannot let your baby go home until we get to the bottom of what's happening here.

MARY   Even if I didn't do it?

WORKER   Even if you didn't do it. Until we know what's happened, we cannot allow your baby to go home. That is the bottom line.

While getting to the "bottom of the injuries" is the agency's primary goal at this point, it doesn't have to be the first thing discussed in the interview. The worker has taken some time to build the relationship with Mary, and then pursues this matter gently, avoiding confrontation. He begins by asking Mary if she understands Dr. Peterson's position about what might have happened rather than take the more confrontational approach of asking Mary how the injuries happened. This draws out Mary's position, that she can't understand how anyone could injure Jayne, which the worker acknowledges. At the same time, the worker is quietly but firmly insisting that the injuries must be talked about and that the baby cannot return home until there is an understanding about what has occurred. Mary's goal, to have the baby go home, continues to be the "leverage" for further discussion.

MARY   So how are you going to find out when I say I don't know? I *don't* know. I wouldn't lie to you, *I don't know*, I don't know how it happened. So if I don't know and I look after my baby well, then how are you going to find out? Who else is going to know?

WORKER   Well, do you think George might know?

MARY   He might. Yeah, he might know something. (*Mary is very quiet at this point.*)

WORKER   Before we go into that, can I just get an idea about how serious you think the injury is? Let me see, on a scale of 0 to 10, where 0 means the injury is not serious at all and baby can go home, and 10 means it's very serious and medical treatment is a necessity, what number would you put on it? Do you understand what I'm asking?

MARY   Yeah, about a 2 or 3. You know, she hasn't cried much, so it's hard for me to say.

WORKER   If she had cried and looked like she was in a lot of pain, where would put the number?

MARY   Oh, probably about a 5.

WORKER   Would anything else have made you feel that it was more serious?

MARY   Well, Dr. Peterson said it's a crack. Now, if she'd said, "The baby's got a broken arm," I would have thought that was serious. That might be more than a 5. That might be 7, because I broke my arm when I was a kid and that did hurt. I thought that a crack is not serious. Do you know what I mean?

WORKER   Did you realize that a fracture is a form of a break?

MARY   No. I thought it was just a crack.

WORKER   Can I just draw this for you? *(Worker draws a diagram and shows it to Mary.)* A break would go clear across the bone, you see? A fracture is basically a break going lengthwise.

MARY   Oh, so it probably did hurt her a lot.

WORKER   Now, this is going to be a hard question. How serious, from 0 to 10, do you think these three injuries, the healed ones on the ribs and the fracture to the arm, would seem to me?

MARY   Well, I suppose you'd probably go right up to 10, wouldn't you?

WORKER   Yeah. Maybe not quite 10. If they were all breaks, then 10, but maybe only 8 or 9. Knowing that a fracture is a form of a break, how much more serious do you think it is?

MARY   Yeah, it seems more serious now. Probably the same as you now.

WORKER   Do you have any idea why I might think it is so serious, and why Dr. Peterson thinks it's so serious?

MARY   I don't like to talk about her being hurt.

WORKER   Would you like to take a break now and maybe go and get your baby and bring her back, and then we could talk some more?

MARY   Yeah, that would be good, but she might cry. You wouldn't mind?

Mary becomes very adamant that "I wouldn't lie to you, I don't know." Showing flexibility again, the worker makes the decision to change the subject a little to prevent a standoff. The worker has made small but significant progress on two of the three immediate progress goals from the assessment and planning form (page 105): He is beginning to build a positive relationship with Mary, and he is discovering her explanations for the injuries. The worker then moves to the third immediate goal: understanding the significance Mary attaches to the injuries. The scaling question and subsequent dialogue serve this purpose very well, and the discussion creates an important shift in Mary's perception of the severity and significance of the fractures.

The worker begins the discussion by establishing and gaining an understanding about how she sees the fractures, instead of putting Mary on the defensive by trying to directly persuade her that the injuries are serious. Inviting her to consider another perspective creates a common understanding. The worker keeps the fact that Mary finds the discussion about the injuries stressful in mind. He shows her that he is sensitive to her feelings by suggesting a break. At the same time, he also gives her the chance to get what she said she wanted at the outset, namely, to be with her baby. In many small, skillful, incremental ways, the worker is carefully building a cooperative relationship with Mary.

Taking a break during interviews is a well-known strategy in family therapy that causes clients to be more receptive (de Shazer, 1988). A break also allows the worker to think more clearly. It is not always possible to take breaks in child protection interviews, but we encourage workers to do so when it is.

Having established a more common understanding of the injuries, the worker immediately brings the discussion back to their cause after the break.

WORKER Okay. Now we've got to do this carefully and slowly so you understand everything. Would you like me to tell you why I think it's so serious?

MARY Yeah, okay.

WORKER The bottom line for us, and the reason Dr. Peterson and we think it's so serious is simply that those fractures could not have happened accidentally. The baby could not have done those things to herself.

MARY So somebody did it on purpose then?

WORKER Not necessarily on purpose. Would it help you if I told you of other examples of where babies have had these sort of injuries?

MARY I suppose so.

WORKER Sometimes things get hard on parents, especially with new babies, and they do things they normally wouldn't do, like being rough and pulling the baby, squeezing it too hard, or shaking the baby when they're really tired and frustrated. So whether it's deliberate or it happens in the heat of the moment, the consequences are the same. Babies can be badly injured, sometimes even die, when these things happen.

MARY But if I didn't do it—and I didn't do it—why isn't she safe with me?

WORKER My view at the moment is that you love your baby and care for her as best you possibly can. As you say, you are learning. But this has somehow happened to Jayne without you knowing about it. Are there times when you are not with the baby?

MARY Like I said, when I go shopping, she stays with George.

WORKER Yes. What other times are you not with the baby?

MARY Well, sometimes he goes and gets her at night if she wakes up, and he brings her to me, but that doesn't happen much now.

WORKER Okay, now this is hard. Can I ask you a real hard question?

MARY Yeah, okay.

WORKER Do you think it's possible that George might have done this?

MARY He could have, but I don't know. He wouldn't hurt her. I don't really believe that George would have done it.

WORKER Do you mean he wouldn't do it deliberately?

MARY Yeah, he wouldn't deliberately hurt her.

WORKER Do you think that he might have accidentally done it?

MARY I suppose he could. But I'm sure he wouldn't hurt her deliberately.

WORKER It's going to be really important for us to talk to him.

The worker has Mary fully engaged in an explicit discussion about the injuries. This is a very significant achievement. Although the cause has not become evident, this should not overshadow a recognition of the worker's skillfulness. The careful discussion in this section opens up a number of possible explanations for the injuries, and the worker has deftly raised the possibility that George may have been responsible. The worker is demonstrating a willingness and flexibility to consider various explanations, and Mary is participating with him in thinking about how these injuries might have happened.

In the next section, the worker decides that further discussion about the injuries will not be productive and changes tack before he overplays his hand. He moves the conversation onto the fourth immediate progress goal: arranging to meet with George.

WORKER   Would it be okay to ask you a few questions about George so I know a bit more about him before we meet?

MARY   Yeah, I dunno what I can tell you about him though.

WORKER   Let me start with this question. On a scale of 0 to 10, where 10 means he's really happy about his life and it's going the way he would want it and 0 means it's a total disaster, where do you think he would rate himself?

MARY   Oh, God.

WORKER   What?

MARY   I was just thinking he's probably over at the disaster end.

WORKER   Really?

MARY   Yeah. I never thought of it like that. But that's probably what it's like for him.

WORKER   His life isn't the way he would want it to be. What would he rather be doing?

MARY   Oh, he'd like to be out with his friends, and go to clubs, and things like that.

WORKER   So he would like to be going out to clubs and having a good time?

MARY   Yeah.

WORKER   What other things would he like to be doing?

MARY   Hmm. Oh, that's about it. He used to have a motorbike, but he had to sell that so we could get a place. That didn't make him very happy, I can tell you.

WORKER   Would he want to be working?

MARY   Yeah, I think he would. But he wanted to go to tech school and do an apprenticeship.

WORKER   So what made him decide that he would go and get a job?

MARY   We had to get our own place.

WORKER Do you think he'd use the word "disaster" to describe his life?

MARY Oh no, he'd use a real swear word. I mean, he's a nice guy, George, don't get me wrong. But his language is not that beautiful. You know what I mean?

WORKER Okay, I get the picture that he's not really happy at the moment.

MARY Yeah.

WORKER Thanks for that. What I'd like to do now is take another break. I'm going to call George at work and ask him to come in. After that, I'll have to talk things over with my supervisor and then, hopefully, meet with you and George together. Is there anything that we've talked about that you'd prefer I didn't share with George?

MARY I don't think so. He's got to know what's going on too.

WORKER Sure, that's important.

The worker gained a little advance information about George from the initial intake information. Before meeting George, it was important to gain some insight into this young man and how he sees life. The information Mary has provided achieves this and increases the worker's understanding of the young couple's life together.

Investigation Interview with George

WORKER Thanks for coming into the hospital. I guess you're wondering what this is all about? *(no acknowledgment from George)* Do you know what's been happening since Jayne was brought to hospital this morning and why we needed to talk to you?

GEORGE No.

WORKER Okay. Let me tell you who I am, what has happened with Jayne, and what Mary and I have been talking about. Is that okay?

GEORGE S'pose.

WORKER First off, I'm John Browning. I'm a social worker with Family and Children's Services. Do you know about the department?

GEORGE Yeah, I been to juvenile court when I was 13 for stealing a bike. My old man told them he thrashed me for that, so I got off with a warning.

WORKER   Really? I want to get down to why we've asked you to come in today. Is that okay? *(no response from George)* We've been called in by the hospital because they have some serious concerns about your daughter, Jayne. As you know, Mary brought Jayne into the hospital this morning because she wasn't well. Is that right? *(George nods.)* When the doctors examined Jayne, they discovered that she has a fractured arm. Did you know that? *(George shakes his head.)* On top of that, X-rays of Jayne show she has had two other fractures to her ribs that are about six weeks old. The hospital was concerned about all the fractures because no one seems to know how they happened. When that happens they call us in because we are the child welfare department and we look at these kind of serious situations.

GEORGE   What's that got to with us?

WORKER   Can I be straight with you?

GEORGE   Yeah, okay.

WORKER   Good. Okay, your baby has three fractures, two old ones and one new one, and the doctors know that she could not have done them to herself. The fractures are serious, but when no one knows how they happened it is even more serious. Does that make sense to you?

George's answers are very limited, and it is important to think about how to get him talking a little more. In this sort of situation, we encourage workers to notice any subjects that get him to open up, to set their sights low, and to consider themselves successful if they can get George to respond with several successive, sentence-length answers.

GEORGE   Look, I don't have much to do with the baby. You'd better ask Mary. She'd know more than me.

WORKER   We have talked to Mary. It's important that we talk to you now.

GEORGE   Are you saying I done them? Is she saying I done it?

WORKER   No, we are not saying that you *or* Mary has done it, and Mary has not said that either. We'd tell you if she said that. The big problem for all of us is that we can't let Jayne go home until we get to the bottom of these fractures and we are sure she is going to be all right.

GEORGE   Well, I dunno. I dunno anything about it. Look, I've got to go back to work soon. How long do I have to stay here?

WORKER   You can leave now if you want to, but I am going to have to talk more with you at some stage about Jayne. I reckon we'll need about another half-hour. Do you have the time now?

GEORGE   Yeah, I s'pose.

The worker makes careful use of his authority to gain George's cooperation. The worker is clear that further talk about the injuries is required, but also offers George the choice of leaving. Despite being shown respect and given choice, George feels that he is being accused. In this situation, it will be hard for the worker to remain open-minded. It would be easy for the worker to focus on George's defensiveness and begin to judge him as the guilty party.

In the next section, the worker attempts to open up the conversation. He shifts the focus of the interview to things Mary has told him about George.

WORKER   Mary said that the baby has really changed your lives, and not necessarily for the better. I hear you had to sell your motorbike.

GEORGE   Yeah. I had to sell the bike for rent and things before I got the job.

WORKER   What's the job?

GEORGE   Office cleaning.

WORKER   Do you like it?

GEORGE   Nah, it's pretty boring, but I need the money.

WORKER   Mary was telling me what you've done for her and the baby, like giving up tech school and selling your bike. Did you know she appreciates what you've done for her and Jayne?

GEORGE   Nah, she never tells me that. She's always going off on me when I want to see my friends.

WORKER   Is that right? You're pretty young to be supporting a family. How has it been? Better or harder than you thought it would be?

GEORGE   Oh, it's been okay, I s'pose.

WORKER   Yeah? What have you liked about it?

GEORGE   Not much.

WORKER   Which bits do you like?

GEORGE   S'pose me and Mary being together. But the trailer's crap, and so's the job.

WORKER   I asked Mary how she thought you would rate your life at the moment, on a scale of 0 to 10, where 0 is it's the pits and 10 is it's the just the way you want it to be. What do you think she said?

GEORGE   I dunno, pretty low I s'pose.

WORKER   Yeah, she guessed it at 0. What's been the toughest part for you about setting up a family?

GEORGE   Oh, the money side's been hardest, and you just can't do anything when you have a baby. I just want to take off sometimes. When I do, she gets in a huff.

WORKER   Yeah. Do you spend much time with Jayne?

GEORGE   Not much. Mary's better at that, I hate all that baby stuff.

WORKER   Have there been any bits you have liked?

GEORGE   I dunno. I never get enough sleep.

WORKER   Yeah, that can be a real hassle. I'd like to talk more about Jayne's fractures now. Do you understand why the hospital is concerned and why they called us in to talk more with you and Mary about the injuries?

GEORGE   No.

The worker moves away from the direct talk about the injuries and explores what this young man's goals might be for himself and his family, attempting to find a way to engage with George and understand how he sees his world. This section also shows how signs of safety questions can actually provide information about possible danger. George is unable to give any real answers to inquiries about what he likes about his family and the baby, and this seems to be generally indicative of the broader frustration he feels with his life.

However, while George is a young man of limited words, he is starting to open up. For example, George has acknowledged that he doesn't really enjoy the "baby stuff." Playing on George's increased openness, the worker brings the conversation back to the issue of the injuries.

WORKER   Okay. Do you know what I mean when I say fracture?

GEORGE   Yeah, it's like a crack in the bone.

WORKER That's exactly right. So it's pretty serious, especially in a young baby. Jayne has a fracture to her arm and two old ones to her ribs. Those fractures could not have happened without a lot of force being applied to her bones. Babies can't do that to themselves. It could only have been done by an adult, either accidentally or deliberately. Since you and Mary don't know how it happened, we have serious concerns about Jayne going home. Do you understand?

GEORGE Yeah. You think I done it, don't you?

WORKER I don't know how it happened. Guessing isn't going to help, but I have to be up-front about what I do know. I know these fractures didn't happen by themselves. I know that having a small baby around can be very tiring and frustrating. I know that sometimes, when things get rough, people do things they normally wouldn't do, like shaking a baby or squeezing it too hard when it's been crying nonstop. I know that these fractures are serious and Jayne can't go home until we all know she is going to be safe. We can't risk something worse happening to Jayne. She can't defend herself or talk about what's happened to her. We need to get to the bottom of it and do something to make sure she's safe. Does that make sense to you?

GEORGE Yeah, but what can I do about that, man? I've told you I dunno anything about it.

WORKER Do you think it's possible you or Mary could have hurt Jayne without knowing it?

GEORGE Well, sometimes we both get a little mad when she's just being, you know, naughty, but I wouldn't hit her, not like my old man done to me.

WORKER So you wouldn't want Jayne belted like you were? (*George nods.*) You know these kinds of fractures don't happen with hitting. They are more likely to happen with a baby being pulled roughly by the arm or shaken or even being squeezed too tightly when changing a diaper. It's more force than just a straight hit, and it can happen by accident. Do you think that could've happened for you?

GEORGE (*George is obviously thinking. He pauses and speaks quietly.*) No.

WORKER   Look, I'm not here to accuse you of anything, but we
         do need to sort this out before Jayne can go home. I'm
         going to call my supervisor now and talk about what to
         do next, and then I'll let you and Mary know. I'd like
         to talk to you both about that.
GEORGE   Yeah. She won't like leaving the baby here.
WORKER   Yeah, I can see that. I'll take you to Mary now and then
         I'll be back in about 15 minutes.

George is now engaged in the discussion, although still insisting
that he isn't responsible for the injuries and that the worker
is blaming him and/or Mary. Unlike Mary, George has a good
understanding of what a fracture is, and this last section of the conversation has made him stop and think. He has also revealed
that he was beaten, probably quite badly, by his own father. Building
cooperation between the service recipient and worker in child
protection investigations often entails being sensitive to when
an issue has been taken far enough. Both Mary and George have
participated in serious and frank discussions about the injuries.
These were clearly discussions that neither of them enjoyed. Pursuing further discussions about the injuries at this point is unlikely to
achieve anything more, but may escalate defensiveness and frustration.

There are many practical matters to be dealt with, and it is
important that both parents understand what is going to happen.
Therefore, the worker makes the decision to take a break, giving
the parents time to regroup and himself time to talk to his supervisor.
In this way, he hopes George and Mary will still have the energy
to understand and participate in making plans for the immediate
future.

The worker has made significant progress on all four of the
immediate progress goals set out in the assessment and planning
form. This is more than enough for the worker to feel good about
the interviews he has conducted with Mary and George.

Building the relationship with the service recipient begins with
the investigation and develops continuously over the course of the
child protection intervention. Each case is unique. The investigation
must be tailored to fit the individuals involved. Consequently, there
is no recipe of questions or single method that will guarantee success.

Partnership in child protection empowers parents to participate in decision-making. Workers can encourage parents to enter into partnerships by offering choices, giving information, and consulting them at each step in the process. We will discuss ways in which case planning is affected by this partnership in the next chapter.

CHAPTER SEVEN

Developing a Cooperative Case Plan

Thorough child protection casework demands detailed, accurate information. This is essential to building a cooperative relationship and developing plans that are tailored to each case. For example, in the case of Mary, George, and Jayne, we know that Mary wants to learn more about babies. This is useful to know, but not nearly enough information on which to build a good plan. The worker must learn what Mary is interested in learning about babies, how she would like to go about the learning process, how she thinks such learning will affect her parenting, and how willing she is to take steps in this direction. Eliciting and understanding Mary's ideas at this level of detail *will* make for good planning, and Mary's commitment to the decision is likely to be strong.

Far too often, young parents like Mary are faced with case plans that include mandatory parenting or child development courses. The professionals involved think classes are a good idea but don't bother to ask what the parents want. Professional-led planning of this sort is usually a recipe for noncompliance or participation based on a sense of obligation. In the end, this will bring about little change in parenting behavior. The statutory agency is not obliged to pursue any of the service recipient's ideas arising from the signs of safety process, but it is always worth remembering that it will be easier to implement the family's suggestions than options generated by professionals.

The signs of safety approach attempts to involve the service recipients as much as possible in case planning. As we have listed in Turnell and Edwards (1997, p. 187), case plans should:

- Clearly articulate the statutory agency's goals for the case in terms of what constitutes enough safety for the case to be closed.
- Incorporate the family's strengths and resources as much as possible.
- Encourage things the family already does to create a safe environment, and draw upon identified exceptions.
- Include the family's own safety ideas as much as possible.
- Draw on the family's general goals if there is a likelihood that they will increase the child's safety.
- Always use those people who are willing (and able) to take action.
- Wherever possible, be presented in the context of family members' goals and aspirations and their position regarding the problem.
- Incorporate compliments where family members are already moving toward their own goals or goals of the agency.

APPLYING COOPERATIVE PLANNING
TO THE CASE OF MARY, GEORGE,
AND JAYNE

Once a child has been removed from its family, as in the case of Mary and George, the tasks facing the child protection worker escalate. Agency protocols and legal requirements regarding alternative care must be fulfilled, meetings usually need to be held with those providing alternative care (institutional or foster), numerous reports need to be written, and so on. These tasks can easily become all-consuming, but it is crucial that the worker and the statutory agency find time and create structures to involve the parents in what is transpiring. Thoburn et al. (1995, p. 217) show that there is a clear link between better outcomes for children and greater involvement of parents. In their study, parents were actively involved in 65% of cases where the outcome was good and only in 35% where it was considered poor or there was no change.

It is clear that a working partnership with George and Mary, reflecting the cooperative case planning attributes described above, has not yet been achieved. Developing a working partnership with this couple will require considerable focus and careful work. It is rare for such partnership to manifest fully in the very early stages of child protection cases if significant statutory power (such as removing a child from its home) is used. However, the investigation and initial meetings are crucial in setting the tone for the casework that will follow. Hence, it is vital to listen carefully to the parents, communicate the possibility of choice, and introduce the notion that their input and ideas are important.

Before the worker leaves the hospital, it is important that he develop an immediate safety plan for Jayne, which is the fifth immediate progress goal set out in the assessment and planning form (p. 105). At this stage, since Mary is overwhelmed and George is pessimistic, the most important aspect of involving Mary and George will be to make sure they fully understand what is happening.

Joint Interview with Mary and George

WORKER   I can see that this has been a difficult morning for both of you. Neither of you would have expected any of this to have happened. (*Mary nods.*) There are some important decisions to make now, and I want to make sure that you understand what I have to say. Is there anything that you would like from me at this stage?

MARY   I just want to find out what's going to happen.

WORKER   Okay, let me get to that. I've talked to my supervisor and the hospital staff. We know that you love your baby, and she means a lot to you. However, the problem is that we don't know how these injuries happened. With three fractures already, our main worry is that something even more serious might happen. We can't let Jayne go home until we are sure she will be safe from further injury.

The worker acknowledges the shock of an investigation while communicating that the situation is serious and involves important decisions. He assumes a position of authority, restating firmly and clearly that the baby cannot go home until safety is assured.

MARY   But she will be safe with us, won't she, George? We never leave her with anyone. You can come and see her every day. You said I looked after her. Why can't she come home? I'll bring her to the hospital. I want her to come home.

WORKER   I can see how upsetting this is for you. Some of your ideas will certainly help us in the future, but for now we can't allow Jayne to go home. I've got kids myself, and I can appreciate your reaction. I'd be devastated if this was happening to me. It's a very hard situation, but these are the rules. Is it all right if I go on? *(Mary nods.)* I have to explain a couple of things to you. Until we find out what happened and are assured of Jayne's safety, I'm afraid she can't go home with you. Now I know that is going to be distressing. *(Mary nods and begins to cry.)*

MARY So you are going to take her away?

WORKER *(Nods and pauses)* We would like you to agree to Jayne's staying in the hospital for another 24 hours. The hospital staff has assured me that they have a place for one of you, probably Mary, to stay in the hospital with Jayne. Tomorrow I want to meet with you again to discuss other arrangements for her care, which I'll tell you about now.

MARY What do you mean—"other arrangements?" Do mean she can't come home from the hospital?

WORKER At the moment, no she can't, but we do want to sort this out with you so that she can.

McCallum (1995) discovered that showing genuine compassion and understanding about the trauma of a child protection investigation and an appropriate degree of self-disclosure were worker characteristics that were highly valued by service recipients. "Conveyance of compassion, commitment and concern, along with respect, is regarded by parents as being indicators of whether or not a worker can be trusted" (1995, p. 4). This is a difficult task in a child protection investigation, but the worker is building these aspects into the relationship without compromising his authority or projecting blame onto the parents.

MARY Oh, this is a nightmare. When can she come home? I don't know what else to tell you.

WORKER I can't set a date right now. That's going to depend on what we can sort out together. Let me explain what we would like to see happen in the next 10 days. Today and tomorrow we would like Jayne and Mary to stay in the hospital so that the doctors can check on Jayne's arm. We would like you to agree to that voluntarily.

Tomorrow I would like to meet with you again to arrange a short-term foster placement for Jayne until we can have what is called a case conference . . .

MARY   Oh God, why did this have to happen? I should never have brought her in. Everything would've been all right. Now you're taking my baby away from me. (*turning to George*) Why don't you say something? You're in this too, you know.

GEORGE   There's nothing to say. They've made up their minds. You think we done it, don't you?

WORKER   I can understand why you're saying that, but the problem is that we don't know how it happened. That's the difficulty we have with Jayne going home. But even if we did know, we'd still have to be sure of her safety. That's why we've got a lot of work to do. Does that make sense? (*no responses*) I need to explain a couple of other things about this situation so you are clear about what we are asking you to agree to. Okay? I would like you to voluntarily agree to Jayne's staying in the hospital tonight and going to short-term foster care tomorrow. You don't have to agree. But if you don't agree with this, I will have to take out a court order for temporary care for Jayne. In that case, you can attend court with a lawyer and contest what we want to do with Jayne. Do you understand what I mean when I say contest?

MARY   Yes.

WORKER   And what we are asking you to agree to?

MARY   Yes.

WORKER   If you agree now but change your mind and try to leave the hospital with Jayne, the doctor will call the police and our 24-hour emergency team, who will come straight to the hospital. I know this is hard, but is that clear so far?

MARY   Yeah. You want me to stay in the hospital for another day and then you want us to agree for you to put her in foster care.

WORKER   That's right, for about 10 days until we can have a case conference with you and decide what to do next. Of course, you can contest this action. I would strongly recommend that you seek some legal advice. If you like, I'll give you a phone number where you can get legal assistance. (*Mary nods.*)

Throughout this sort of discussion, it is important that the worker proceed slowly. By the end of this section, it is clear that Mary understands what will happen, even though she does not like it.

MARY Can I see her?

WORKER Most definitely. We would encourage you to spend as much time with Jayne as you can.

MARY What about her clothes and things?

WORKER Yes, that's important for Jayne too. We will need to arrange all that tomorrow. I would also like to learn about her routine so that the foster mother can do the things you normally do with her, and, hopefully she won't be too upset either.

MARY Yeah, she can get upset if you don't do things her way.

WORKER I'll let you talk about this for a few minutes and decide what you are going to do. Is there anything else you'd like to know at this stage?

MARY No, it's all just a blur right now.

WORKER Sure. I'll just be outside if you need me to go over anything again.

Mary begins to think about the practical consequences of foster care. It is important to give her an immediate sense of involvement in the placement as she begins to offer her ideas. She is demonstrating that she is trying to cooperate with the plan and thinking of the best for Jayne. In a very small way, this is the beginning of a "working coalition" (the term used by Farmer & Owen, 1995) between the parents and the agency.

MARY This is going to be hard, but we'll sign the paper for her to stay in the hospital. I want to call the legal people to hear what they say before I sign the foster paper.

WORKER Sure, that sounds very sensible. Is there anything else that you'd like to tell me right now, or anything you would like to know?

MARY No.

WORKER Okay. There are two more things I'd like to ask. First of all, I was wondering is there anyone who could support you through this, either family or a friend?

MARY Probably my aunt.

WORKER Maybe you could get her to come to the hospital. I think it would probably help you to have someone to talk all this through with.

MARY Yeah. It'd be okay for her to be here too?

WORKER Of course. Now the second thing may sound a bit strange after all we've talked about. I certainly don't expect you to have an answer straight away, but I want to raise the issue of Jayne's safety before we finish here. Because her return home is going to depend a lot on knowing that she will be safe, do you have any ideas about how you could show us that Jayne will be safe at home?

MARY Well, George reckons you've made up your mind, don't you *(George nods)*, so there's not much point in trying to show you anything.

WORKER Okay, that's a tough position for us all to be in. So maybe we have to show you that we are genuine about Jayne going home once we sort this out and know she will be safe. How could we show you that we actually do want her to go home?

MARY I dunno, I can't think anymore. *(pause)* Maybe you could let me take her out for a while.

WORKER You mean once she's in foster placement? *(Mary nods.)* That certainly sounds like a reasonable request. That's possible. It looks like we all have some hard thinking to do to sort this out together. I'll have to ask you to sign some papers now, and then let's finish. I'd like to meet with you again tomorrow, early in the afternoon. Is that okay?

MARY Well, I'll be here.

WORKER What about you, George? Is 1 p.m. okay with you?

GEORGE Yeah, that's all right.

WORKER Right. If you want to clarify anything at all, please call me at this number. I'll give you an after-hours number that I can be contacted through if needed. Otherwise, I'll see you tomorrow.

The worker facilitates a useful shift in the conversation by inviting Mary and George to start thinking more overtly about safety. He also indicates to them that they have to work together to sort out the problems. The agency will have to demonstrate to the parents that it is genuine about working with them to return the child home.

Unless the agency can prove its intentions, the parents will remain defensive.

Some readers may be irritated by the attention given to the small achievements and fine detail of the casework in the face of such a serious case. However, big solutions rarely resolve these cases. It is the small increments of careful interaction that are the fundamental building blocks of creating cooperation between worker and family.

UPDATING THE ASSESSMENT AND
PLANNING FORM

The updated assessment and planning form (p. 139) recognizes that the case has advanced in a number of small but very important ways (all listed on the safety side of the equation):

- Point 22 details that significant collaboration has begun with Mary. This is evidenced by the modification of her views about the seriousness of the injuries and the fact that she has listened to the worker's input and contributed ideas regarding the foster placement.
- Although she did not like talking about the injuries, Mary discussed the issues in a meaningful way. This is also a sound start to building a constructive working partnership (point 23).
- Mary spontaneously offered that she wants to learn more about caring for babies (point 24).
- Although the relationship between the worker and George isn't ideal, it has commenced and George has discussed the issues (point 25).
- It is important to recognize that for a man of his age, George is making significant efforts to support his family (point 26).
- Finally, the parents have voluntarily agreed to the first stage of the immediate safety plan, Jayne remaining in hospital for the next 24 hours.

At the same time, the investigative interviews have highlighted other aspects of the situation that contribute to the potential danger in the situation:

- It appears that the family is fairly isolated (point 21), although this has not been systematically explored.
- George is unhappy with his life, his job, his income, and his lack

of freedom. He has nothing favorable to say about parenthood in general or Jayne in particular (point 20).

- Both parents are defensive, and George particularly feels that he is being blamed for the injuries (point 19).
- Point 18 notes the fact that the cause of the injuries remains unknown. This is an issue that must be addressed.

The Issue of Denial

The greatest concern to any child protection worker in this case would probably be that the cause of the injuries is still unknown. Mary is adamant that she would never hurt Jayne, but has conceded that George may have done so. George is resolute that he knows nothing about what has occurred, but is increasingly defensive and feels that he is being blamed.

The traditional and dominating view in child protection (e.g., Dale et al., 1986; Bentovim, Elton, & Tranter, 1987) asserts that cases in which there is denial of responsibility are essentially unworkable and untreatable. Adopting this logic means that child protection becomes organized around the issue of denial, and the worker focuses on trying to get the parents to admit responsibility for the maltreatment. This will often lead to a sullen standoff between the parents and worker, an occurrence that is well-known to child protection agencies the world over. These all-too-frequent cases tend to result in a stalemate between the agency and the family. Planning options become limited to one of two extremes: either the case is closed due to the lack of any capacity to create change, or removal of the children (permanent or extended) is pursued.

Casework is more productive when professionals organize their thinking around safety, specifically around building sufficient safety for the child to remain in or return home. The worker has greater latitude when acknowledgment is not the only avenue through which progress can be made. It is cases like this that demonstrate how the radical nature of a safety-focused child protection approach can help to diffuse the family-professional standoff in cases of denial of responsibility.

Lusk (1996) has made a careful study of acknowledgment and denial in child protection. He argues that the issue of culpability, which is embedded in Judeo-Christian ethics, is a cornerstone of the western legal process. For example, a guilty plea at the outset of a trial will commonly reduce the defendant's sentence. The idea that denial indicates untreatability (first reified in Freud) is central

Mary, George & Jayne: Postinvestigation.

Signs of Safety Assessment and Planning Form

DANGER ⟵ ⟶ **SAFETY**

(You may wish to spatially locate items between the danger and safety poles along this continuum)

List all aspects that demonstrate likelihood of maltreatment (past, present, or future).

1. Baby has fracture to left arm.
2. Baby has healed fractures on ribs, indicates history of injury.
3. Baby aged 7 months.
4. Mary says she doesn't know how injuries happened.
5. Mary becomes withdrawn when issue of fractures discussed.
6. Mary not aware of injury, discovered by local doctor.
7. Mary took 3 days to bring baby to hospital.
8. Mary seems ignorant of injury and its significance.
9. Mary and George are both very young parents.
18. Following investigation, cause of injuries still remains unknown.
19. Parents defensive, (particularly George) feel blamed.
20. George is frustrated with his life and dislikes parenthood.
21. Family seems to be isolated from immediate family and other supports.

List all aspects that indicate safety (exceptions, strengths and resources, goals, willingness, etc.).

10. Injuries have come to light and baby's health is being monitored by hospital.
11. Mary is attentive and cares appropriately.
12. Dr. describes reasonable bonding between Mary and baby
13. Mary says she loves baby and it "cuddles into her".
14. Baby is clean.
15. Developmental milestones of baby OK.
16. Mary wants to take baby home and willing tostay in hospital while baby cared for.
17. Mary willing to talk to statutory agency.
22. Collaboration has begun with Mary: input from worker has modified her views and she is contributing to placement arrangements.
23. Mary has talked about injuries in meaningful way and was considering various possibilities regarding cause of injuries.
24. Mary spontaneously says she wants to learn more about parenting.
25. A relationship has begun with George.
26. George has been making significant efforts to provide for his family.
27. Parents have agreed to initial plan (24 hr hospital care) voluntarily.

Safety and Context Scale | 3 | 3 |

Safety Scale: Given the danger and safety information, rate the situation on scale of 0-10, where 0 means recurrence of similar or worse abuse/neglect is certain and 10 means that there is sufficient safety for the child to close the case.

Context Scale: Rate this case on a scale of 0 - 10, where 10 means this is not a situation where any action would be taken and 0 means this is the worst case of child abuse/neglect that the agency has seen.

Agency Goals What will the agency need to see occur in order to be willing to close this case?

i. Knowledge of cause of injuries elicited and responsibility taken by perpetrator.
ii. Safety plan in place to protect against any further injury.
iii. Responsibility taken by parents to implement plan.
iv. Implementation of safety plan demonstrated by parents over time.

Family Goals what does the family want generally and regarding safety?

Mary's general goals: i. Care for her child in own home. ii. Be a good mother. iii. Learn more about babies.
George's general goals: i Better job. ii. More income. iii. Increased social life.

Immediate Progress What would indicate to the agency that some small progress had been made?

i. Carefully go over everything again that has happened with Mary and George. Ensure understanding before moving on.
ii. Continue to explore collaboratively the parent's understanding of injuries and possible causes. Avoid blaming.
iii. Improve relationship with George, perhaps connect to him through the violence of his own father.
iv. Work with and involve Mary and George in what needs to be done to ensure safety.
v. Conduct fuller assessment of social supports and extended family support.
vi. Involve significant others e.g. the Aunt.
vii. Build clear, open relationships between all parties including placement agency, foster family, and George and Mary.
viii. Prepare for case conference, maximize understanding and input from Mary and George.

to psychodynamic thinking and is thereby persuasive in the helping professions and, consequently, in child protection. As Lusk writes, "abusers who deny strike at the core of this tradition and at the objective of progress through insight" (1996, p. 15). In his study of 86 child protection professionals, Lusk found that parental denial invariably provokes some sense of hopelessness in workers and frequently results in the feeling that they have no options for working with the family.

Acknowledgment of responsibility is only one means of achieving sufficient safety for the child. Acknowledgment, while preferable, is neither a sufficient or necessary condition of safety. We know of cases where acknowledgment of responsibility has not ensured a child's safety and, conversely, of other cases where safety has been created in families where no acknowledgment has been forthcoming.

Complete or even substantial agreement on the maltreatment and its causes, may not be possible but this does not mean that families and parents will not work toward improving the safety of their children. Our own experience and the work of others, most notably Essex, Gumbleton, and Luger (1996) and Essex and Gumbleton (1999) has shown that it is possible to make significant progress in such cases by building a working partnership that focuses on creating future responsibility and safety.

At the same time, we do not in any way suggest that the agency cease further investigation into the issue of responsibility simply because it has been denied. Clearly, it is an important sign of safety if acknowledgment of responsibility is elicited. Therefore it is still an important agency goal on George and Mary's updated assessment and planning form, but it must be pursued in such a way that it does not become *the* dominant agency goal. That type of investigation could threaten or destroy the capacity to maintain a cooperative relationship between the worker and Mary and George. When the worker and agency recognize that progress can still be made without acknowledgment of responsibility, workers are less likely to be overtaken by a sense of hopelessness and are better able to deal with the family in an open-minded manner.

So far, the interviews have achieved a good balance between investigating the injuries, building cooperation, and creating a focus on increasing safety for Jayne. To maintain this balance the worker must think carefully about how to pursue the issues of denial and acknowledgment further. Interrogating Mary and George may gain an admission, but it is more likely to manufacture antagonism. A more expedient route would be to continue to emphasize the seriousness of the injuries while sensitively utilizing the leverage of having custody of Jayne by indicating that acknowledgment could hasten the child's return.

Workers can also to discuss abuse and injuries in general without direct confrontation. With Mary, this involved discussion about her own experience of a broken arm, which was then linked back to the current concerns. In further interviews with George there is room to broaden a discussion of abuse and maltreatment by focusing on his own abuse at the hands of his father. This may lead toward acknowledgment on the part of George, or may be productive in further enlisting his motivation to keep Jayne safe in the future. At the very least, such a discussion will be valuable to further clarify George's views regarding maltreatment and his apparent position that abuse is equivalent to hitting.

STATUTORY AGENCY GOALS: THE CORNERSTONE OF CASE PLANNING

Case planning needs to be informed by careful assessment of past maltreatment and the likelihood of future harm. However, this traditional process of risk assessment cannot tell workers how to address the risks. Case planning will lack focus if the agency cannot state specifically its immediate and future goals. MacKinnon (1992) found many families subjected to child protection investigations reported that the agency was usually very clear about what the problem was, but family members were often confused or simply did not know what was actually expected of them.

Explicit goals help the agency evaluate its options and communicate its expectations during casework. Frequently, the agency is not explicit with the family because the staff, rather than thinking in terms of what it expects to see, deals instead with what it expects to stop. A focus on the abuse stopping is inevitably a negative focus. It is a focus on what people will *not* be doing, and it is hard to work toward *not doing* something without providing something else to fill the vacuum. On the other hand, a focus on what the agency expects to see happening instead is much more positive and gives everyone involved something to work toward. The parents may not like the goals, but they will have something to aim for.

Setting the Goals in the Case of Mary, George, and Jayne

The agency goals that would allow case closure for Mary, George and Jayne have remained the same in both the initial and the updated assessment and planning forms. These goals are an important focus, but their value will not be fully realized until everyone understands and agrees on what they specifically entail for the parents and the agency. As long as these goals are meaningful only to the agency, their utility is limited. To advance matters, the worker must discuss the goals with George and Mary so that they more fully understand and will work toward what the agency needs to see to close the case. This is the sort of partnership that helps resolve child maltreatment cases.

In considering the parents' goals, we know that Mary wants to bring Jayne home (Mary's general goals, point i., listed under family goals), to be a good mother (point ii.) and to learn more about babies (point iii.). While Mary's goals seemed to be focused in the home, George's goals are focused out in the world: getting a better job, increasing his income, and having more contact with his friends. As yet, overlap between the parent's goals and the specific safety goals of the agency has not been developed. While the issue of safety was put on the agenda in the joint interview, the parents and worker have not yet significantly discussed the building of increased and substantial future safety for Jayne. Mary and George have not yet articulated any ideas that could be called safety goals.

Given the seriousness of the maltreatment, it is most likely that Jayne and her parents will be separated for a significant length of time. To maximize the chances of collaboration, it will be vital to provide full information and explanations to George and Mary (this process began in the transcripted interviews), seek their input wherever possible, and provide them with choices about what will happen (for example, with regard to the location of foster or alternative care, extent of access time, choice regarding access supervisors, and so on). This will demonstrate that their opinions can make a difference, and, hopefully, create a context in which the parents will participate in the development of a safety plan.

It will also be invaluable to draw in other members of the family. Perhaps the most obvious choice is Mary's aunt who has been helping Mary care for Jayne. Any significant others may be able to bring more information to light or offer constructive influence and assistance. Usually, the more people who are involved and know what is happening, the safer the child is.

It takes discipline and determination on the part of workers and supervisors to maintain the focus on building safety. The immediate progress goals in the case of George, Mary, and Jayne reflect this discipline, as evidenced by their explicitness and clarity. These goals explain, in detail, the things that need to happen to move the case toward closure. The eight immediate progress steps toward building a partnership and creating safety in this case are (as identified on p. 139):

i. Meet again with Mary and George and, as the first item of business, carefully discuss and review everything that has already occurred and everything that is being proposed, so that the parents have as complete an understanding as possible of what is happening. Taking the time to go over everything again is a vital aspect of continuing to build the relationship between worker and parents. It demonstrates that the worker is sensitive to the stressful impact the agency's intervention will have had on Mary, George, and Jayne.

ii. As outlined earlier, continue to discuss the injuries and possible causes in a sensitive manner. This should be done as collaboratively as possible, avoiding the creation of a sense of blame or accusation.

iii. It is important to improve the relationship with George. It may well be possible to connect with him through discussing the violence of his own father. This sort of discussion would also begin to address point ii.

iv. Engage Mary and George more fully in discussion and action regarding what needs to be done to ensure safety.

v. Conduct a fuller assessment of social supports and extended family support.

vi. Involve appropriate significant others (e.g., the aunt).

vii. Build clear, open relationships among all parties who are to be involved, including placement agency, foster family, and George and Mary.

viii. Prepare for a case conference by explaining the meeting to the parents and maximizing the input from Mary and George.

Parents whose children have been removed from their care are resentful at the enormous disruption of their lives created by the initial investigation. Afterward, they may feel abandoned; there is frequently no further contact with professionals until the case conference (Farmer & Owen, 1995). So, although it may be difficult for the worker to find the time, the professional must continue to be closely involved at this stage in order to build the working coalition. The parents will be forming their views about the nature of the relationship and what is possible between themselves and the agency. It is crucial for the worker to be directly involved in the development of their thinking and not simply cast them adrift until they meet again at the case conference.

This is as far as we will follow the case of Mary, George, and Jayne. The transcripts and detail associated with this case were presented to demonstrate the sort of careful thinking, decision-making, and action (what some call micromanagement) that constitutes good collaborative child protection practice. Continuing to follow one case at this level of detail would not allow for a full presentation of the signs of safety approach.

Case example

It is important to remember that, even when statutory intervention eventuates, the worker can still build a cooperative relationship with the family. This was achieved in a case where the statutory agency had sufficient evidence to remove an eighteen-month-old child from drug-addicted parents. The parents' two older children had previously been taken into custody. However, rather than act immediately, the agency went through a two-day process of dialogue and careful explanation, canvassing various (small and large) options with the parents. Following this, the officer* contacted the mother, informing her that the statutory agency would be taking the child into its care and asking whether they would cooperate or if police involvement would be necessary.

The parents were upset and angry when the child was removed. Like Mary and George, both parents were denying responsibility and refuting the allegations. However, the careful relationship work paid off, since it created a context in which the parents, of their own initiative, contacted the worker two days after the toddler was removed. They were now offering several of their own proposals. In a subsequent meeting, the parents displayed much more engagement with the process and new, mutually agreed-upon plans were created.

In this case, the removal of the child triggered the mother to leave the relationship. She moved to the country to reside near her own family. The mother requested that the same caseworker

---

*Joe Fleming

continue to assist her. Even though the worker had to travel a considerable distance, well beyond the geographic boundary covered by his office, the statutory agency granted this request, feeling that it was important to support the mother when she was making such a serious attempt to redirect her life. This demonstrated to the woman that the worker and the agency took the partnership seriously and that she could influence the process.

With considerable support from the extended family, the worker elicited the mother's own goals and was able to help the woman become drug-free (the first goal of the agency before return of the children was to be considered). The woman found employment and established a home of her own. After about six months, when the mother was stabilized in her new life, she consented to work with the regional office closest to her home. Subsequently, the youngest child was returned to her care.

Developing a fit between agency and family goals: A case study

The logic behind the signs of safety and its focus on goals is fairly straightforward and commonsense. However, that does not mean that the implementation of the ideas is simple. In fact, careful and thorough work is needed to utilize the approach well, as the following case demonstrates.

This case involved a blended family with four children, the oldest of whom had arrived at school with a bruised eye and a scald mark on the chest. The child frequently came to school unwashed and displaying signs of neglect. When visited, the family provided explanations for the injuries that, while not completely conclusive, were believable, and there was no discrepancy between the stories of the child and the parents. The injuries were more indicative of neglect and lack of foresight by the parents than active abuse, and this concern was echoed in the living arrangements of the family and the fact that there was evidence of neglect with all the children.

The family lived in the cellar of an abandoned, condemned commercial building. The building posed numerous, serious hazards to the safety of the children. The worker* realized that little could be gained by disputing the parents' explanation for the physical injuries. Instead, he skillfully utilized his understanding and acceptance of the explanations as a platform to point out the school's concerns regarding the eldest daughter's cleanliness. He then explored with

---

*Joe Fleming. This case is also described in Fleming (1998).

the parents what they could do to prevent further complaints from that source. This left the issue of the hazardous building as the most pressing concern.

Local authorities wanted to evict the family. It would have been feasible for the worker to use the agency's authority to pressure the family to move out (in fact, some workers within the agency argued that this was the best way to proceed). The worker, in consultation with the authors and with support from his superiors, pursued a more cooperative line, though still clearly maintaining that the agency's preference was that the family find alternative accommodation.

The worker carefully and gracefully drew the parents' attention to the hazards in the cellar, in part through inviting them to rate on a 0–10 scale the extent of the danger within their home. The worker was very pleased to discover that the parent's own rating was 6. Although the worker's own rating may have been a point or two lower, this created a platform to discuss specific concerns regarding the hazards. The upshot of these discussions was that the father fixed or rectified many of the problems. In several of the subsequent home visits, the father was able to proudly show his achievements to the worker, who promptly complimented the man on his efforts. It is important to note that many of these problems were identified by the local government inspector, but prior interventions had only provoked an oppositional response from the parents.

Further discussions resulted in the family purchasing a trailer to provide better housing for the children. In conjunction with this, the worker wrote a letter supporting the family in their plans to continue to live on the site. Again, it is worth noting that there were concerns raised within the statutory agency about whether the worker should pursue such a path, as the letter could be seen to align the agency with the family, "against" the local government officials. The worker took the view that it was a constructive way to enhance and demonstrate his partnership with the family. It is worth pointing out that this family had a history of involvement with the statutory agency and that previous workers, the school, and the council had a very negative perception of the parents. It was not always easy for the worker, but he persisted and made progress as he carefully worked to build bridges between the agency's concerns and goals and those of the family.

The worker maintained the pressure of statutory intervention to initiate the changes, while skillfully eliciting and utilizing the family's own ideas for resolving the problems. Asking the parents to provide their own scaled assessment of safety/danger was instrumental, not only in that it laid the foundation for discovering what the parents wanted to work on, but also because it showed the worker that the parents, approached in the right way, were able to acknowledge the problems. This case also required patience on the part of the worker. To him, the hazards in the cellar were obvious, and he would have liked to have addressed issues more speedily, but restraining his own impatience allowed the parents to take charge of the process and make changes at their own pace. While this necessitated going slowly, the parents' ownership of the process made their children safer in the long term.

CHECKING THE FAMILY'S PERSPECTIVE:
CONFIDENCE, WILLINGNESS, AND
CAPACITY REVISITED

Any plans, however they are developed, should be discussed in detail with the family members. They are the ones who are most affected, and very often they are expected to implement plans. Unfortunately, an atmosphere of sullen acquiescence all to often becomes dominant when parents and children feel they have no choice but to agree with the professionals. In this environment, families may even give their assent to plans they have no intention of implementing, inevitably leaving the worker dismayed. An antidote to this phenomenon can be created by checking all plans with family members before they are committed to paper to openly clarify the family's willingness, confidence, and capacity to implement.

After weighing the family's perspective, the agency must make a judgment as to its own confidence regarding the family's capacity for implementation before it accepts any ideas as part of a case plan. This may include generating its own confidence scales.

If the agency proposes a course of action that did not originate from the family's ideas, it is crucial to explore the family's position, confidence, and willingness regarding the proposal. This will decrease the likelihood of noncompliance and demonstrate to the agency how useful its ideas seem to family members (who, after all, are the ones supposed to change as a result of implementation). For example, if the agency is thinking about asking the father to move out of the family home for a period of time, the agency should first learn the opinions of the other family members. If parents are being asked to go to counseling or a parenting course, the worker should canvass their willingness to participate and learn what would constitute a constructive counseling experience or parenting course for them.

The agency may decide that the urgency of a situation necessitates immediate action, in which case there is no time to discuss the possible impact of statutory intervention upon the family. However, if possible, discussion with the family prior to this sort of action will most likely be useful. For example, if a father beats his children severely, considering it his right to do so, the officer might ask, "Would it make a difference to you if you knew we were going to take you to court if you continued to discipline your children in this way?" When children are to be removed, wherever possible at least, the children can be asked, "What difference would it make if you lived somewhere else?" Prior to such interventions, broader discussion with other members of the family may be valuable. Sooner or later the statutory agency will most likely have to commence negotiations about the possibility of the child returning home.

It is also important to be mindful of an individual's capacity to undertake a given plan. For example, if a woman has a partner who is very controlling, she may believe that a particular course of action would make a difference, but feel completely powerless to implement it. Attending a parenting group may seem straightforward to the worker and still feel outside the realm of possibility for a parent with feelings of inadequacy in groups or major logistical difficulties with transport or childcare. These sorts of things might seem obvious, but unless child protection workers discipline themselves to open-mindedly canvass all plans with service recipients, implementation will rarely meet expectations.

The Family Does the Planning

To conclude this chapter, we will consider a detailed case study showing what one family achieved on its own after antagonistic relationships had developed between the family and the professionals. The professionals were convinced that the problem would only be resolved through intensive one-to-one counseling with the two young people involved and significant statutory intervention. This focus on the professionals' own solutions had overwhelmed any attention that might have been given to building a cooperative relationship with the family and to focusing on day-to-day safety.

This case involved James, a sixteen-year-old boy, who was initially charged in relation to a sexual relationship he had with an 18-year-old, intellectually handicapped woman. The information available to the statutory agency at the time of referral came from the police and treatment agency involved (see the assessment form on page 151). When the police originally investigated the matter, they discovered that James's 13-year-old sister, Sally, had witnessed some of the incidents for which her brother was charged. In interviewing Sally it was discovered that there had been sexual contact between the two siblings and, as a result, James was also charged for these incidents. James maintained that he was not guilty of the original charge, asserting that the activities were mutually consensual. Although he denied the allegations regarding Sally for a day or two, he soon admitted to them and took responsibility by accepting that he was in the wrong. As a consequence of not contesting the charges relating to his sister, he was incarcerated for a short time and then mandated by the court to participate in a live-in treatment program for sexual offenders that resulted in him being separated from the family for several months.

James and Sally were also sent to a specialized sexual abuse counseling service where they were seen separately. The professionals did not want James to return home following his time in the residential program. However, no alternative accommodation was arranged for him following his discharge. This plan, although intimated to the parents, had never been an item for mutual discussion. The family had no placement options; all of the extended family lived in other states. Since the parents were committed to James and no other options were available, they brought him back to the family home.

The sexual abuse counselors and the police were convinced that the family was protecting the perpetrator, who would reoffend against Sally. The treatment professionals described the family as "hostile," "lying about events," and "minimizing." In conjunction with the police, the matter was referred to the statutory agency for immediate intervention. Based on the vehemence with which these concerns were expressed, the statutory agency formed the view that either James or Sally needed to be removed from the home using statutory power.

At this stage, two workers (one to investigate the matter and another, more senior practitioner) who were familiar with the signs of safety approach became involved with the case. Instead of taking the police on the initial visit, the worker* made the decision to

---

*Elizabeth Soronsen

undertake the home visit on her own. Although the case plan was to remove one of the siblings from the home (see form p. 151), she was trying to be open-minded about the matter. With her knowledge of the case, the worker rated the amount of safety in the situation at 2 out of 10 in the context of a case that had a seriousness of 3 out of 10.

Sitting down with the parents, the worker was surprised to discover that the family had done many things to ensure their daughter's safety. Firstly, the parents had spelled out to James that he would have to leave home immediately if Sally ever felt uncomfortable about him and/or if the abuse recurred. James and Sally were never alone; an adult was always present. The worker saw that the parents enforced this rule and that the children also enacted the rule themselves. The parents also rearranged work and holiday schedules to make sure the plan was put into effect. Another part of the family's plan was to alter the sleeping arrangements in the house to separate the siblings' bedrooms. The parents explained to the worker that they supported both of their children, but that they would not allow sexual contact to occur between them again.

When interviewed alone, Sally stated that she rated her safety at 8 out of 10 because the plan was working, other people knew what had happened, and she knew she would be believed if she reported anything happening in the future. Sally rated her confidence that the plan would continue to work as 9 out of 10.

Armed with this information, the worker faced the problem of convincing her superiors that there was sufficient safety for both children to remain in the family home. The signs of safety assessment process was particularly beneficial at this point, since the worker was able to lay out the new information (see form p. 153). This detailed her changed assessment of the safety, which she now rated at an 8 in a case seriousness context of 5. The plans for the case changed, as reflected in the agency goals on the second form. It was decided that the case could be closed if the safety plan was being maintained, up to and one month beyond completion of the court case relating to the intellectually handicapped young woman. It would also be necessary that Sally continue to report experiencing the same level of safety.

A major problem in this case involved the complete breakdown in relations between James and Sally and their respective sexual abuse counselors. James was particularly antagonistic about the experience,

Jarnes and Sally: Postintake.

Signs of Safety Assessment and Planning Form

(You may wish to spatially locate items between the danger and safety poles along this continuum.)

DANGER

List all aspects that demonstrate likelihood of maltreatment (past, present, or future).

1. Sexual offences (2x penetration) by James 16yo against 18yo intellectually handicapped young woman.
2. James's sister Sally (13yo) witnessed abuse.
3. When interviewed Sally discloses to police she and James have engaged in simulated sex, mutual masturbation and oral sex. James was sent to juvenile prison on these charges.
4. James is back in family home with Sally after his release.
5. Family position is that the activity was consensual (minimizing?)
6. There is no relationship between parents and professionals.
7. Police and treatment agency are saying parents are hostile, lying about events, minimizing significance, protecting the perpetrator.
8. Treatment agency say James can readily intimidate Sally and she is at high risk; that one or other must leave the family home.
9. Family has experienced huge disruption from whole process.

10. James has admitted offences but says they were consensual.
11. Sally and James both attending treatment but Mother appears to be controlling process by always attending with them.
12. Family isolated from extended family in Victoria

SAFETY

List all aspects that indicate safety (exceptions, strengths and resources, goals, willingness, etc.).

10. Sally is generally okay at school.
11. Parents want both children.

Safety and Context Scale   2   3

Safety Scale: Given the danger and safety information, rate the the situation, the situation on a scale of 0-10, where 0 means recurrence of similaror worse abuse/neglect is certain and 10 means that there is sufficient safety (for the child to close the case.

Context Scale: Rate this case on a scale of 0 - 10 where 10 means this is the worst case of child abuse/neglect and 0 means this is not a situation where any action would be taken and 0 means this is the worst case of child abuse/neglect that the agency has seen.

Agency Goals What will the agency need to see occur to be willing to close this case?

• Sally to be safe from reabuse, probably with Sally and James permanently separated.

Family Goals What does the family want generally and regarding safety?

• Have both children in the family home.
• Get professionals out of their lives.

Immediate Progress What would indicate to the agency that some small progress had been made?

• Remove Sally from family home or get James living elsewhere immediately.

saying he was being treated "as an offender, not as a person." Similarly, Sally felt she was only being seen as a victim. The worker aimed to build bridges between the young people and their counselors, but in the end Sally discontinued counseling, feeling very disgruntled about the whole experience.

James began to see an independent psychologist instead of the sexual abuse counselor. Initially, the psychologist had to work very hard to build James's trust, but once this was achieved the therapy was productive. After seven sessions, a report was prepared wherein the psychologist expressed the view that there was minimal likelihood that James would reoffend. The worker was not satisfied when she read this report, because it had little specific detail to support the judgment. As a result, the worker asked the psychologist to submit a new report documenting the signs of safety that justified her judgment.

As discussed earlier, professionals are usually capable of generating detailed reports regarding maltreatment and the dynamics surrounding such events. However, the same level of detail is often absent in reports proposing sufficient safety to close a case. The worker who is familiar with assessing and interviewing for safety may have to assist other professionals in detailing elements indicative of safety. Thus, the worker led the psychologist through a discussion of exactly what she was observing that satisfied her regarding James. The psychologist was then able to prepare a second report that provided a sound and detailed basis for the assessment.

The worker maintained contact with the family during and beyond the period of the final court appearance, all the time monitoring that the level of safety for Sally was being maintained. During this period, Sally reported feeling that her level of safety increased. When the court case was heard James was found to be not guilty of the charge relating to the 18-year-old. The judge had agreed that it was a consensual relationship. Approximately one month after the court hearing the statutory agency closed the case.

Hindsight in such cases always makes things seem more obvious. The significance of the worker's actions should not be overlooked. In this context, it is worth relating some of the things that the parents talked about when one of the authors went to obtain permission from them to publish details of the case. The entire process had placed extraordinary strain on all members of the family. Up until the child protection worker became involved, and apart from the relationship

James and Sally: Postinvestigation.

Signs of Safety Assessment and Planning Form

(You may wish to spatially locate items between the danger and safety poles along this continuum.)

DANGER

List all aspects that demonstrate likelihood of maltreatment (past, present, or future).

1. Sexual offenses (2x penetration) by James 16yo against 18yo intellectually handicapped woman.
2. James's sister Sally (13yo) witnessed abuse.
3. When interviewed Sally discloses to police she and James have engaged in simulated sex, mutual masturbation, and oral sex. James was sent to juvenile prison on these charges.
4. James is back in family home with Sally after his release.
5. Family position is that the activity was consensual (minimizing?)
6. There is no relationship between parents and professionals.
7. Police and treatment agency are saying parents are hostile, lying about events, minimizing significance, protecting the perpetrator.
8. Treatment agency say James can readily intimidate Sally and she is at high risk; that one ex other must leave the family home.
9. Family has experienced huge disruption from whole process.
10. Sally is generally okay at school.
11. Parents want both children.
12. Breakdown in relationship between treatment counselors and James: they want to confront him with offenses and him to take full responsibility. James feels he is being treated as a sex offender not a person.
13. Treatment agency continues to believe scale is 2/3.
14. James and Sally have told statutory worker that they were sexually abused in Victoria, but relationship with treatment service not sufficient to explore this there.

SAFETY

List all aspects that indicate safety (exceptions, strengths and resources, goals, willingness, etc.).

15. Family open and willing to talk with and work with statutory worker.
16. Family rules and strategies for safety are in place:
17. For example; if Sally made uncomfortable &/or if abuse recurs James must leave house. James and Sally never allowed to be alone together, an adult must always be present. Parents police this carefully; and witnessed to do so. Sally and James understand and enact both rules themselves. Parents reorganized James & Sally's bedrooms to different ends of house. Special Christmas holidays arrangements made since parents couldn't be available. Parents supportive of both children.
18. Sally rates her safety at 8 and confidence of maintaining plan at 9 because: People know what has happened; nothing move has happened since Jame's return (5months); Sally would tell immediately if something did happen and knows she'll be believed.
19. Worker established two outside adults Sally could safely and quickly tell if she has concerns.
20. James has told his mother he will never do it again.

Safety and Context Scale   [8 | 5]

Safety Scale: Given the risk and danger information, rate the situation on a scale of 0-10, where 0 means recurrence of similar or worse abuse/neglect is certain and 10 means that there is sufficient safety for the child to close the case.

Context Scale: Rate this case on a scale of 0 - 10 where 10 means this is not a situation where any action would be taken and 0 means this is the worst case of child abuse/neglect that the agency has seen.

Agency Goals What will the agency need to see occur to be willing to close this case?

- Close case once changes re 18yo are dealt with in court (hearing to commence in one month) assuming family has maintained safety plan throughout and one month beyond trial.
- At this point all family members confident implementation of safety plan will continue.

Family Goals What does the family want generally and regarding safety?

- Have both children in the family home with Sally's safety assured.
- Get professionals out of their lives and get on with their lives.

Immediate Progress What would indicate to the agency that some small progress had been made?

- Statutory agency to articulate closure goals to family and treatment agency.
- Foster better relationship between treatment agency and Sally and James.
- Bring treatment agency's views closer to statutory agency's and family's.
- Establish in detail with James what makes him certain he will not reabuse.

with one policeman, the family's experience was that all the professionals were antagonistic toward them. The family members were subjected to a number of humiliating experiences at the hands of professionals. For example, the parents were told by several professionals that they were unfit and unprotective parents and that the abuse was all their fault. The family remained angry about these and other events. Their greatest complaint was that they felt no one was listening to them.

Asked what would have happened if, as was initially proposed, the child protection worker had arrived at the house in the company of police and forcibly removed one of the children, the father reflected that he would probably have become aggressive and perhaps even lashed out. The parents went on to reflect that, in this scenario, their son would have become more withdrawn and depressed, blaming himself even more not only for the sexual offenses, but also for destroying the family. They felt that the marriage relationship, which was already under great strain, may well have broken at this point.

It is often easy to overlook the family's experience of the investigations. Except for the openness of the worker and her determination to hold the option of statutory intervention in abeyance while she canvassed the family's views, a bad situation could have become very much worse. At the very least, forcing one of the siblings out of the home would have resulted in the case dragging on and tying up many, many hours of professional time while hostility escalated between the family and agency.

What had transpired in this case before the child protection worker became involved was simply the consequence of paternalism in action. The professionals were of the view that they knew best and were not interested in the family's perspective. Collaborative planning is almost impossible in these circumstances. Using the signs of safety approach and her willingness to listen and elicit the family's perspective and plans, the child protection worker reversed this process. The case planning process immediately became much more straightforward.

For many child protection workers, this approach to case planning seems overly simplistic. In this regard, it is worth considering the New Zealand experience in utilizing family group conferencing, which we described briefly in chapter 1. This model is probably the most radical and sustained experiment in eliciting service recipient's own plans. In over 85% of cases in which this model is employed, the statutory agency is able to collaborate with the family's own plans without reservation (Marsh, 1996). This is a remarkable statistic in a field used to professional-led planning, especially since family group conferences are only convened with substantiated cases of a serious nature. However, families and parents are not able to participate and contribute to planning unless there is a genuine openness and a structural commitment by professionals and their organizations to be responsive to the families' ideas. Further guidance in this regard is provided in literature such as Ban (1992, 1993), Keys (1996), McCallum (1992), Mayer (1989), Scott and O'Neil (1996), Morris and Tunnard (1996).

While case planning is usually not as straightforward as in the case we have just considered, the important message to take out of it is to recognize that carefully and genuinely eliciting the family's own best plans will always be a valuable undertaking in child protection casework.

CHAPTER EIGHT

Maintaining the Focus on Safety: Ongoing Casework and Treatment

The ultimate aim of all child protection work should be to create safety for the child, preferably within the natural family. The signs of safety approach seeks to keep this obvious focus in the front of the worker's mind. Maintaining this focus throughout ongoing casework should also clarify the appropriate time to close the case.

FOLLOWING UP, ASSUMING NOTHING

In chapter 2, we proposed the principle that workers restrain the urge to make judgments, particularly before they have listened carefully to the perspectives of family members. It is similarly useful for workers to limit their expectations (expectations being a form of judgment) of what the service recipients will or will not do. Even where family members have participated actively in the generation of a case plan and have demonstrated their willingness to work with the agency, the more cautious approach of assuming nothing is usually beneficial. When workers restrain their expectations, they are unlikely to be disappointed if the family is unable or unwilling (for whatever reason) to implement plans. Assuming nothing allows the worker to notice improvements that do occur and to be sensitive to changes that arise from unexpected circumstances. By keeping expectations in check, the worker becomes less invested in a particular outcome, remains flexible, and is less prone to frustration and pessimism.

Restraining expectations also allows for the reality that many families involved in child protection services live in vulnerable circumstances and, even with the best of intentions, may not be able to achieve what they and the worker hope for, or have committed themselves to. In our experience, parents who have not achieved what was planned will often feel defensive, expecting to be criticized by those in authority (an experience they may well have had previously). Workers who can restrain their own expectations and maintain a perspective of openness toward the person will likely be able to avoid appearing critical and, therefore, have a greater likelihood of being helpful.

Case example

The following case displays just these attributes in a situation that would have frustrated many professionals.

A woman was referred for treatment to a colleague* as a court requirement for regaining custody of her six-year-old daughter. This women had been discharged from prison a year previously following her prosecution for contributing to the death of her one-year-old son (interestingly, the courts allowed her to have custody of a new infant son after her discharge). The child protection worker had interpreted the mother's reluctance to engage in treatment for a year after release as an indication that she didn't really want to regain custody of the older child.

When treatment began, it indeed seemed that the worker might be right: even though the woman talked enthusiastically about wanting the daughter back, she failed to appear for her second appointment a week later. She reappeared after three months, communicating the same degree of enthusiasm and many excuses for her disappearance and failure to complete other court requirements. She missed the next appointment and again reappeared three months later. This time, there were some changes for the positive: she had finally completed the parenting classes and found a suitable apartment. Subsequently, she complied with the court requirements of treatment, even admitting that she had made a mistake in the death of her infant son, something she had refused to acknowledge in prison. At this time she had also reconciled with her own family, whom she had fallen out with during the period leading up to the death of her child. She discussed and settled issues with her parents

---

*Larry Hopwood

regarding her previous boyfriend and abuse she herself had suffered at the hands of a family member.

When this women was seen with her daughter, our colleague was struck by their close relationship, evident verbally and nonverbally, despite several years of separation. Both mother and daughter were attentive and positive toward each other and expressed trust that the other would do the right thing. The mother also demonstrated her capacity to care appropriately for the baby she had been allowed to keep. For example, when the baby suffered a prolonged illness that was not appropriately dealt with by the local children's hospital, the mother assertively and determinedly pursued additional treatment to resolve the problems. The daughter was subsequently returned to her mother's care, and six months after the end of treatment the child protection worker informed the therapist that the mother and daughter were doing fine.

Our colleague's patience and openness contributed significantly to the progress made in this case. Many professionals would have become frustrated with the nonattendance and noncompliance of the mother and withdrawn their involvement. Our colleague, though, was willing to wait, keep an open mind regarding the woman's motives, and cooperate with the woman's own timing.

Throughout this book we have argued that good child protection practice is undertaken by workers who can squarely face the realities and ugliness of the alleged or actual maltreatment without dehumanizing or demonizing the people involved. This requires a receptiveness and open-mindedness about the people involved that allows for possibilities and change without minimizing the level of harm or risk. These are the attitudes that will help a child protection professional proceed slowly and assume nothing. Though this sort of approach is often learned through many years' experience, we are continually encouraged and inspired by experienced child protection workers who retain and extend both a clarity of purpose and an openness of attitude. The following case demonstrates these attitudes.

Case example

A girl in her early teens (whom we will call Gail) was raped by her stepfather's brother (Alan) while on a camping trip. The mother, Helen, had not participated in the weekend's activities, but immediately recognized that something was wrong when Gail returned home. Helen made her daughter sit down and talk, and in this way she found out what had occurred. At the same time, Gail also revealed to her mother that her stepfather (Thomas) had been sexually abusing her for the past two years. Helen immediately confronted Thomas and demanded that he leave the family home. Following this, a member of the extended family notified the child protection service.

Helen was terrified when the child protection worker* first visited. Her previous experience of "the welfare" had been negative and she was scared that all her children would be removed. (Gail was the eldest of four. Bill, her full brother, was two years her junior, and the youngest two, both preschoolers, were Thomas's natural children.)

The case was further complicated by long-standing antagonism in Helen's extended family: Several relatives viewed her as an unfit parent and, on several occasions, had reported her to the child protection authorities. This was in part fueled by the fact that Thomas had fathered a child with Helen's sister. It was the sister who initiated most of the reports.

On the first home visit, the worker entered the messiest house that she had encountered in her many years' experience. She found a family and mother with a highly chaotic lifestyle. Being sensitive to the signs of safety, the worker acknowledged that Helen had already made significant efforts to improve Gail's safety. The worker was very mindful of Helen's fears of "the welfare" and was careful to compliment Helen on her commitment to her children, the manner in which she approached her daughter such that the girl was able to reveal the rape and abuse, and her determination in forcing the abuser to leave the family.

It was evident that the shock of the events had caught up with Helen, and she was too overwhelmed to discuss things at any length. The worker did, however, ask both Helen and Gail to rate their sense of Gail's immediate safety. Both indicated she was quite safe for the time being. Drawing on all the information, the worker decided that there was enough safety for her to end the interview and schedule another appointment for a few days later. Following that first contact with the family, given the seriousness of the disclosures, the worker judged the level of safety for Gail at 3 (10 meaning safety is certain, 0 meaning reabuse is certain) with a case context of 2.

---

*Caroline Sullivan

In the second contact with Helen and Gail, the worker discovered that Thomas had returned several times, ostensibly to visit his own two preschool-aged children, when Gail was home and no other adults were present. The worker acted quickly to forbid this situation, in part because Gail's own safety rating of these occasions was 1 out of 10.

It is important to note that the worker did not intend to be guided solely by Gail's answer to the scaling question. The answer simply provided her with good information and reflected that Gail appraised the situation realistically. If Gail had rated her safety in that context as high, the worker, would have been alerted to another problem. She still would have ensured that Thomas had no access to Gail, but she would also have set about gently exploring the issue further with the teenager. Following this second interview, the worker immediately met with Thomas. Together, they modified the visitation arrangements so that the girl would not be left alone with her stepfather again and ensured that there would be supervision for all visits with the younger children.

In subsequent contacts, the worker felt it was vital in building a collaborative relationship to address Helen's fear of the removal of the children. The worker informed Helen that if she continued to ensure Gail's safety in the same ways that she had already demonstrated she could not see herself having to remove any of the children. The worker also made it clear to Helen that she would do everything she could to help her maintain her focus on protecting her children and helping Gail deal with the abuse. Continued safety would eliminate any need to act on the complaints emanating from Helen's sister and other members of the family.

The worker's efforts to engage and reassure Helen clearly hit the mark; Helen revealed that she had been abused as a child. When she had disclosed the detail of this abuse, her mother had not believed her. In contrast, Helen was determined to provide the best support she could to Gail. Helen also commented that she had previously suspected that Thomas might have been abusing Gail, but when she asked, Gail had denied it.

The worker built relationships with Helen, Gail, and Thomas, always focusing carefully on building and maintaining safety for the teenager. She regularly visited the family home and made a careful choice to not confront issues such as the mess of the house since, although the state of the house was of concern, she judged that to raise it directly would be counterproductive. Further, the state of the house was not hampering Helen in supporting Gail and ensuring her safety. The worker was also careful to assure herself that the developmental milestones and general behavior of the two younger children were acceptable.

At the outset, Helen was very cautious about taking the matter to the police. When she had been abused as a teenager, she had gone to the police and they did not believe her story. The worker spent considerable time talking through this issue with both Helen and Gail. While the worker notified the police of the situation following the initial report, it took six months before both mother and daughter were ready for Gail to make a statement against Thomas and Alan.

Throughout the case, the worker continually elicited the mother's own concerns about Gail and the other children and encouraged her to come up with ideas to deal with these issues. In this way Helen addressed the chaos of her life and the mess in the house and began to deal with these things. The worker complimented Helen whenever she made any progress toward her goals.

The worker also took the time to build a good relationship with Gail, monitoring the teenager's sense of her own life, the sort of support she wanted, and her own sense of safety. The worker would often drive the teenager home from a group for sexually abused young people as a way of keeping in touch in an informal context.

A remarkable aspect of this case is that the worker developed a cooperative relationship with Thomas. The worker gained an admission of the sexual abuse from him well before Gail and her mother were ready to take the matter to the police. The worker skillfully utilized this knowledge to get Thomas to keep Gail safe by staying away from her. When the police became involved, the worker had a significant influence, getting Thomas to admit the abuse to the investigating officer and enter a guilty plea in court (for which he was subsequently jailed for six years). Thomas did this in part to spare Gail the trauma of a police investigation and cross-examination in court. The worker facilitated these actions on Thomas's part by giving him time to tell his story and not continually challenging his position that the abuse wasn't really his fault. The worker felt able to do this because she judged that Thomas's confession gave her sufficient leverage to ensure the safety she was seeking for Gail.

The worker also continued to keep Thomas informed as issues arose. She took the man seriously in his desire to have a meaningful relationship with his natural children and indicated that if this was done with demonstrable safety for the children—primarily to be shown through supervised contact—she would be supportive. Throughout her contact with this man, the worker was direct with him regarding the problems and situations of risk and was likewise very clear about what she required and expected. In child protection casework, it is not unusual for workers to sidestep working with perpetrators, but this case demonstrates that it is possible to work collaboratively and productively with men such as Thomas.

This is a very serious case with complex family dynamics involving fragile, fearful, sometimes aggressive, and confused individuals. Skillful, careful, and purposive use of her child protection role helped the worker facilitate cooperative relationships and assist significantly in securing very good outcomes for Gail and the other children. With the support of the worker, Helen made many changes in her life: she brought the relationship with Thomas to a complete end, she became more decisive and better organized in her life and in her care of all the children, she entered a relationship with a man that was more positive for her than any she had previously experienced, and she began to take more pride in her own appearance and that of her house. The worker complimented Helen at every step. The outcomes for Gail in this case were very good. She was making good progress in her life.

Not everything in this case progressed as the worker would have liked. It became obvious that Gail's brother Bill, who was a few years younger, was deeply affected by everything that had transpired. He was clearly very angry, sullen, and withdrawn much of the time, and Helen was very concerned about him. It was eventually discovered that he had also been sexually abused by Thomas on several occasions. Attempts were made to draw Bill out of his shell, but, despite the best efforts of the worker and Helen, he remained largely uncommunicative. Additionally, at the time of writing, the matter of the rape inflicted by Alan was only just coming into the courts. The worker was not willing to close the case until she had seen the family make a successful transition through the stress of the court case.

Through the many case examples in this book, we have demonstrated that good child protection casework builds on an openness to the people involved and a careful focus on detail. The caseworker involved with Helen, Gail, and Thomas displayed exactly these qualities, and her careful work made a significant difference for the family.

TREATMENT, NOT THERAPY: AN IMPORTANT DISTINCTION

The heart of the signs of safety approach is its focus on goals: both the family members' and the statutory agency's. This focus has important consequences for ongoing casework and treatment. Ideally, the fundamental goal of mandated child protection work is to make the situation safe enough for the child to remain in or return to the family home. This sort of purposive focus on safety is exemplified by the efforts of the child protection worker in the case just mentioned. In many cases, however, the ongoing work of dealing with abuse or neglect issues occurs (or is meant to occur) in "therapy." We put therapy in quotations since we believe that services that are provided by therapists or counselors to open child maltreatment cases should be called "treatment" and not described as therapy at all.

Therapists have an ongoing debate among themselves as to how they should exercise their role with families in which children are at risk. Notable family therapists like Haley (1980) and Boscolo, Cecchin, Hoffman, and Penn (1987) are of the view that any form of "social control" has no place in the therapy room. This seems to suggest that therapy cannot be conducted with families where child protection issues are current. Others, for example, Furlong (1989) and MacKinnon and James (1992a, b), believe that therapy is an appropriate service to be provided to statutory cases. They argue that all therapy is a value-laden and involves a power differential (the therapist being more powerful).

There are, in our view, very real and important issues to be addressed here. For example, by and large, therapists are trained to be "nonjudgmental." The tradition of interactional brief therapy that informs the signs of safety model and on which we base much of our practice has as one of its fundamental premises the notion that the therapist adopt a nonnormative stance regarding the behavior and goals of the client. Nonnormative means brief therapists "use no criteria to judge the health or normality of an individual or family. As therapists, we do not regard any particular way of functioning, relating, or living as a problem if the client is not expressing discontent with it" (Fisch, 1988, p. 78). However, it is completely inappropriate to adopt a nonnormative stance toward the maltreatment of children. It also seems obvious to us that all professionals, whether charged with statutory obligations or not, have a responsibility to children in actual or possible situations of abuse and neglect to make judgments regarding their safety. This could be construed as "social control," but we would rather view it simply as responsible professional practice.

The pragmatic reality for many therapists involved with child protection cases is that their services are being paid for by the statutory agency. The latter, however the professional describes the service, will inevitably require verbal and/or written reports regarding danger, safety, and overall risk. Therapists working with child maltreatment cases will not only have to make these judgments, but they frequently also have to exercise some amount of coercion or leverage to maintain the involvement of family members in the treatment process. This is something that is essentially foreign to the notion and practice of psychotherapy.

Therapy as we understand it is a process designed to assist clients to focus on and achieve what *they* want. A therapist providing service to a family with which the statutory child protection agency maintains an involvement cannot focus exclusively on what the client family wants. A successful service in this situation needs to take into account the goals of the statutory agency as well as those of the client family.

Further, therapy is informed by the pursuit of ideals such as personal growth, self-actualization, healthy family functioning, well-being, insight, and increased awareness. These goals are pursued in a therapeutic milieu that is often described as empowering, enabling, or even liberating.

Child protection casework and any treatment process attached to it should have as its primary goal the achievement of family functioning that is safe enough for the statutory agency to close the case and get out of the family's life. Figure 8.1 and table 8.1 further illustrate our perspective.

The diagram describes a continuum. The left hand side represents children in danger within a family. The right hand end of the continuum represents a family functioning "ideally." Between these two extremes lies the critical statutory child protection goal: family functioning that enables the child to be "safe enough." This is the

FIGURE 8.1

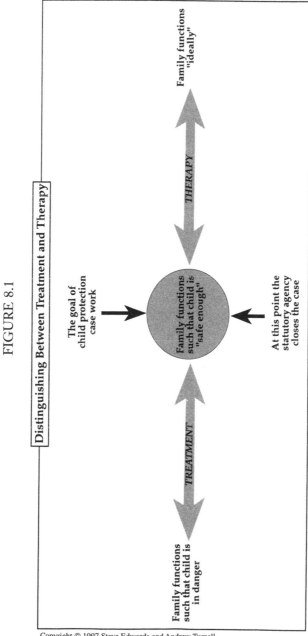

Distinguishing Between Treatment and Therapy

Family functions "ideally"

THERAPY

The goal of child protection case work

Family functions such that child is "safe enough"

At this point the statutory agency closes the case

TREATMENT

Family functions such that child is in danger

TABLE 8.1
Distinguishing Therapy from Treatment

	Therapy	*Treatment*
Objectives	Well-being, insight, growth, self-actualization, healthy functioning.	Pragmatic focus on creating sufficient change to build enough safety to close the case.
Goals	Essentially defined by the client.	Defined by the service recipient and the statutory agency. Requires close collaboration with the statutory worker since they are crucial to defining what "enough safety" looks like.
Service user	Designed for voluntary clients.	Designed for service recipients.
Professional role	Facilitator focused on what client wants.	Therapist's skills of joining and listening are required, and the professional also needs to be comfortable exercising some level of social control and leverage.

point where the statutory agency should close the case. Services provided to assist a family to move from a situation where a child is in danger to the point where that child is adjudged to be "safe enough" should be described as treatment, since this will involve a process of matching family and agency goals. The space between "safe enough" and ideal family functioning is the territory of therapy, since herein only the family's goals need to be attended to.

It is not unusual for therapists and counselors to become bogged down with child protection cases because they are pursuing ideals of functioning that arise out of the ethos of middle-class therapy. Typically, this manifests itself in trying to get child protection service recipients to display highly self-reflective levels of insight, analysis, or acknowledgment that may or may not increase safety for the maltreated child. This is part of the difficulty that was operating in the case of Sally and James (chapter 7). The sexual abuse therapists involved in this case were seeking to achieve levels of insight and understanding in the two young people that completely overlooked the fact that their family was already functioning to create a safe environment for Sally.

Using the term "treatment" rather than the term "therapy" reminds professionals that they cannot simply follow the philosophy and ideals of the field of psychotherapy when dealing with child protection cases. This is a pragmatic (if not entirely theoretically pure) distinction that enables professionals to be clear with themselves and the service recipients about what they are doing. That is, the service they are providing is about creating increased safety for the children in an environment where powerful others (the statutory agency, its workers, and also the treatment professional themselves) will make independent judgments regarding the level of safety that has been and could be created.

By describing as treatment the service delivered by a therapist to assist a family to become safe enough, we are, in part, seeking to move beyond the therapy/social control debate. We are also attempting to make the task of the treatment professional more straightforward and transparent. We are advocating that all professionals involved in the delivery of services in child protection cases must be purposefully involved in achieving safety for the child. Consequently, treatment professionals and statutory child protection workers need to work in close collaboration.

Given that the goal of treatment provided by any therapist or counselor should be to achieve "enough safety" to satisfy the statutory agency, we would discourage therapists from taking on child protection cases where the worker wants to hand over responsibility for the case. MacKinnon and James (1992a, b) describe a treatment approach tailored specifically for child protection cases. They are careful to describe how they actively and purposively involve the child protection worker. Close colleagues Susie Essex, John Gumbleton, and Colin Luger from the United Kingdom go further. They are so convinced of the need for close collaboration between the treatment agency and the child protection professionals in their work with cases where acknowledgment for substantiated abuse is not forthcoming that they require the child protection worker to attend each treatment session (Essex et al., 1996; Essex & Gumbleton, 1999).

BOGGED DOWN AND STUCK CASES

Cases often become stuck because the casework lacks a purposive focus. Sometimes the caseworker, the treatment and other professionals, and family members are unsure of what they are trying to achieve. Our first priority when listening to a story of a child protection case that is stuck is to facilitate an assessment of how much safety already exists and what exactly would need to be seen to bring the case to a close.

Case example

This was exemplified in a case in which we both had direct involvement in the removal and the return of the children. In this situation, the children had been removed from a mother who was a prostitute and drug addict. Her care of the children had been erratic and frequently very poor. The children needed to be removed because her husband, who had always been the primary caregiver, had been imprisoned for four years. During the imprisonment, the couple separated permanently; then, upon his release, the father applied for custody of the children.

The process of returning the children dragged out over two long years, complicated by a number of issues, including the man's legal status in Australia and whether or not he had a criminal record in his country of origin. The case was comprehensively reviewed by a senior officer of the statutory agency who observed that, if this man had had custody of these children at the time of the review, there would not have been the slightest possibility of removing the youngsters. He recognized that the children were being held in care due to numerous issues that, while they were important, did not have any direct bearing on the capacity of the father to provide sufficient safety for the children. When the reviewer focused directly on whether this father was capable of providing a safe enough home environment for his children, it was clear that reunification should proceed forthwith. Many other cases throughout this book demonstrate the clarity that can be achieved when the same purposive focus on safety is evident.

Doing Something Different

When cases become stuck, we try to think about them as simply as possible, hence our focus on goals and safety. We find it very useful to apply two basic rules regarding problems and their resolution that are the foundation of brief therapy (de Shazer & Berg, 1995; Fisch et al., 1982). These rules are:

- If what you're doing doesn't work, don't do it again; do something different.
- Once you know what works, do more of it.

In cases that are bogged down, both the family and the professionals are usually stuck in a cycle of repeatedly doing something that is not working.

Two case examples

The mother in this situation worked as an "erotic" dancer and would often travel into remote regions of the country to perform. On some occasions she would take her children with her, and on others she would leave them with relatives or friends. The statutory agency took the two children into its care on the premise that they were being neglected, their schooling was erratic, they were being placed in moral danger, and there had been several incidents of physical abuse when the children were in the care of friends. There were also concerns regarding possible sexual abuse. The children, both under 12, had been in care for almost two years, though the mother maintained regular and consistent contact with them.

The statutory agency wanted the mother to acknowledge the problems of the past and admit that, while living the life of a dancer, she was unable to provide a stable home for her children. They had involved the therapist with the case to achieve this aim. Throughout treatment, the mother would express the view that her problems were all caused by the statutory agency meddling in her affairs. The children took the same view, proclaiming as vociferously as their mother that it was the welfare that was keeping them apart. They were, however, relatively well-behaved, leading a relatively stable life in their foster home. The therapist had asked the mother to rate her relationship with her children and her care of them. She rated both at 8 out of 10. Interestingly, she also gave a score of 8 regarding the care the children received in their foster home.

For the therapist, the situation was particularly unsatisfying and, in consultation, she realized that she was essentially undertaking a holding operation on behalf of the statutory agency. She felt she was being driven by the somewhat unstated goals of the statutory agency to get the mother to face up to the problems of her lifestyle as a dancer. This simply led to the mother being defensive and placing blame on the statutory agency. Not surprisingly, the counselor was frustrated that nothing was being achieved, but wasn't sure what to do. She wondered if the lack of progress was indicative of a lack of her own skill.

It seemed to us that the professionals and family members were caught in a cycle of repeatedly trying to solve the problem with a solution that wasn't working. To change the interactions a little, we invited the therapist to review the case with the mother and find out what she wanted from treatment. It eventuated that the mother felt there was little purpose in the treatment and wanted nothing from the process. The next step that flowed from this was for the therapist to encourage the statutory agency to be clear with the mother regarding what they wanted in the light of the fact that the mother would not alter her lifestyle. Following some discussions, a case conference was convened and a lengthy conversation took place between the mother and statutory agency staff on just these matters. The upshot was that plans were drawn up to make the foster placement a permanent arrangement for the children.

Initiating a process of review based on the views of the service recipients is often very productive in seemingly stuck child protection cases. Hence, we encouraged the therapist to step out of the role of trying to achieve the statutory agency's goals and instead adopt a role of reviewing the case with the mother. After that, the rest became a process of following through with the logic of what the mother stated.

The research of child protection service recipients shows that most have very firm opinions about the services they have received and often enough have clear ideas about the sort of help that would be best for them. Relationships in child protection cases are not like those in most other helping relationships, where the service recipient can just walk away. Not surprisingly, the consumer will inevitably have a view, often a strong one. The caseworker or treatment professional can utilize family members' desires to express their views and engage them in a process where their assessment of progress and ideas are heard.

In another case, a very frustrated worker asked a drug-addicted single mother in a relationship with a violent pusher for her opinion on the progress of the case. The statutory agency had the care of the woman's two children. Asked to assess her own life on a scale of 0–10 the woman admitted she would rate it at maybe 2 or a 3. She went on to acknowledge that she was not really in a good state or situation to care for her children. She was also asked how she assessed the assistance she was receiving from the child protection service. The woman replied that she felt the agency treated her exactly as she was treated by her own mother: they were always telling her what she was doing wrong, something she already knew.

The worker then asked what she could do to help her. Without hesitating, the woman replied that she would like a relationship where the worker acted genuinely interested in her. Although the worker had been aware of some of the woman's perspectives, she certainly had not gained such an overall sense of how the woman saw things. What particularly stood out for the worker was that the woman had a very modest and realistic desire. She was not making big claims, such as immediate return of the children. This provided a new focus for the worker and, over time, the woman's life took on a more positive direction. Eventually, she left the violent relationship.

Admitting That the Case Is Not Progressing Well

There are many ways of doing something different to get stuck cases moving, but two strategies stand out as particularly successful. The first is the process of initiating a service recipient-led review, which we have just considered. The second strategy, where appropriate and applicable, is for the professionals to admit they have been wrong, admit they have missed something, or that they feel that what they are doing is not helping the situation. As with initiating a family-led review, this changes the nature of the power differential between worker and family member somewhat and can serve to rebuild cooperation.

Case example

This approach had a dramatic effect in a case involving a mother, her partner, and their infant daughter. The daughter was found to have a number of fresh and healed injuries and, as a result, the child was taken from the parents' care. Both parents denied responsibility for the injuries. The statutory agency began proceedings to have the child legally committed into its care and indicated it would not consider returning the child to the mother's care as long as denial was maintained and the partner remained in the home. At this point, the partner left the relationship, which distressed the mother greatly. She blamed the statutory agency for splitting them.

The mother was referred to a therapist for treatment with the goal of exploring how the child sustained the injuries and what led up to this. The treatment became bogged down because the therapist could not get the mother to acknowledge the injuries or how they might have occurred. The statutory agency also found itself stuck. Although they wanted to return the infant to its mother, they were not willing to do so until the mother took responsibility for what had occurred. Pressure was also building from another quarter because the couple who was looking after the infant made it known that they did not wish to continue caring for the child. At this point, the caseworker consulted with us.

The thing that stood out for us immediately was the fact that the mother had already given, through her lawyer, a written acknowledgment of responsibility. In this, she stated that she had not been protective and that the injuries had occurred while the child was in her care. While it was not a "complete acknowledgment," the fact that the mother had made this written statement seemed to have gone unrecognized. We wanted to know if the mother herself was wondering why she was being badgered to say it all again. We proposed that the worker meet with the mother and the therapist and begin by saying, "I've called this meeting because I've been reviewing the case, and I think we need to make new plans. Something struck me when I was reviewing the case, something that I don't know why we hadn't seen before, namely that you have already acknowledged that these injuries occurred while the baby was in your care. We had told you that was all we needed to begin thinking about returning the baby to your care. That must have been a hard thing for you to do. Can you tell me how you decided to make that statement?"

This acknowledgment of what the statutory agency had missed broke the ice, and the mother became readily engaged in the ensuing discussions. The meeting moved on to discuss what the mother understood the statutory agency to be looking for and what she understood the purpose of the treatment to be. The discussion then focused on how the mother could demonstrate concretely and specifically that she was able to appropriately care for the baby. Interestingly, and most notably for the worker and therapist, the mother, of her own volition, began to question her relationship with the father in that meeting.

Before the conclusion of the meeting, the mother stated that it was the best meeting they had had and asked why they couldn't have talked like this before. The therapist felt reenergized and had a new direction for the treatment.

Where relationships between the professional and the family have severely broken down, the process of rebuilding is not always this quick. In one case in which we were involved, direct contact was no longer taking place between the family and the agency. In this situation, it was decided that the manager of the agency would write to the family, expressing his regret that things had broken down so badly. He offered to discuss the matter with the parents, perhaps with a view to involving a new worker to make a fresh start. This intervention, the involvement of a new worker, and some careful work over the course of several months brought about some small gains in the case and allowed the parties to start talking to each other again.

CASE CLOSURE

Having built a detailed picture of what safety will look like means that the statutory agency has negotiated with the family what it needs to see, in specific detail, to recognize the child is safe enough for the agency to close the case. Many examples in this book have detailed the application of this principle.

It is the nature of child protection work, however, that there will always be cases where such clarity is not possible. At times, case closure will come about because of more ambivalent motives, for example, a lack of evidence resulting in circumstances where the statutory agency can neither prosecute nor gain leverage and access to the family. In situations where cooperation between the family and agency has not been created, a process of attrition tends to set in over time, and the case grinds to a halt. These sorts of cases will be closed because there are other, more urgent, priorities, and no further allegations have come to light.

There is a tendency in the child protection field to exaggerate the numbers of cases where cooperation is impossible. The English study by Thoburn et al. found that "although some parents and children had such severe problems that it was not possible to involve them at all these were very few in number. Even in circumstances when the degree of difficulty meant that a poor outcome was almost inevitable, some workers did manage to secure some semblance of participation in the process" (1995, p. 229).

It has always been our worst fear that a child protection worker will utilize the signs of safety approach with a family, close the case based on signs of safety that have been created and/or found, and then, subsequently, learn that a child has been significantly injured, abused again, or perhaps killed. This, of course, is exactly the fear that will, at some stage, keep most child protection workers awake at night, worrying whether they have done the right thing. However, up to the time of writing this book, it has not transpired. In contrast, on several occasions when closed cases that utilized the signs of safety approach were reviewed by senior management because of renewed concerns, the feedback has been positive. In one example, a case was re-opened due to fresh allegations, and a senior manager of the Western Australian statutory agency initiated an audit of the file, seeking to establish why the case was closed in the first place. The case had been closed based on a carefully documented list of signs of safety. The manager who reviewed the case was very pleased with the clarity and detail of the case documentation and a message came back to the worker and us that it was very evident why the case had been closed and the action was seen to be very appropriate.

Case closure is a judgment call and, as with all other assessment points in child protection work, it is not unusual for professionals to disagree on the decision. We know of cases that have been closed although we have were uneasy about the situation and, conversely, cases held open with no constructive purpose for continued involvement.

Case example

We were involved in a case providing treatment service to a man who had been convicted and briefly jailed for sexually molesting a six-year-old girl. The man was a refugee from a Southeast Asian country where he had been a peasant farmer and was illiterate in his own language. He understood little if anything about the notion of Western reflective therapy and the case had progressed by very concretely focusing on the things the man could do to make sure he never again molested a child.

At the conclusion of the treatment, which involved six sessions, the man rated himself at an 8 on a scale of 0–10 where 10 indicated he was certain he would not molest again and 0 meant he was sure he would do so. He asserted that 8 was the highest score he would be able to achieve since "nothing can be guaranteed in this life." However, he was as confident as he could be that such behavior would never occur again. His confidence arose from the following: (1) He was avoiding any contact with young girls where there was any possibility of being alone with them and gave examples of leaving situations where this might have occurred; (2) he was more active and had obtained two part-time jobs; (3) he was actively seeking re-unification with his wife and family (his view was that it was being depressed about the break-up of his marriage that had led to the offense); and (4) he was going to a brothel to express his sexual urges.

The man felt he could do nothing further and the treatment should end. We agreed that it was time to close the case, since there was also nothing further we were able to suggest or offer, and to prolong the process would most likely begin to alienate the man. Interestingly, the parole officer was of the view that counseling should continue and was pessimistic about the man not reoffending. However, she was unable to suggest any additional behavioral changes that might occur or what further sessions should focus on. We therefore cooperated with the client and closed the case. The man continued to report to his probation and parole officer for the mandated period. Though she did not agree with our closure of the case, it was disappointing to us that the parole officer chose not to verify the changes the man had reported by contacting his family and pastor, even though the man had indicated to us he would be willing to allow the officer to do so.

Two stuck cases that were successfully closed

The following two examples involve creating the circumstances where the cases could be closed positively. Both examples come from the caseload of the same worker.* The statutory agency had been involved in both situations for protracted periods, there was little collaboration between the family and agency, and the case management required new direction. By focusing on existing and required safety, both cases were brought to the point of closure.

The first case involved a father who had been convicted and jailed for sexually abusing two primary-school-aged children that had been

---

*Dianne Dullard

temporarily in his care. At the time the worker began her involvement the father had returned to live with his wife and their two children, who were of similar ages to those he had abused. The man had been in treatment for almost three years, but, other than personal therapeutic gains, it was inconclusive whether anything had been achieved in this process.

The case was further complicated because it had achieved considerable notoriety in the local community and had been dealt with as something of a "hot potato" by previous workers and managers. The family was ambivalent about the statutory agency and was basically fed up with the agency's continual but inconclusive intrusion in their lives. When the new worker first came to the house, the children greeted her at the door with the question, "Have you come to take us away?"

To prepare for the first meeting with the family, the worker reviewed the signs of safety already evident (though they had not been acknowledged). The worker already knew that there was nothing secret. The mother had disclosed the abuse in the first place, and then subsequent family disclosure had guaranteed that it was very widely known. The worker also ascertained that the children were progressing well at school and were always well presented. In fact, the school was impressed with the achievements of both children, given they came from a family with severely physically disabled parents.

The worker had decided that, on her first visit, she needed to be very explicit with the mother regarding her goals. She made it clear that she intended to establish the current level of safety for the children and establish how the family was achieving this. She also expressed her intention that, if the children's safety was sufficient and clearly demonstrated, she would be proposing that the case be brought to a case conference for the purpose of closure.

To achieve this, the worker asked to meet with the children alone. The mother was very cautious about this, since she had had enough of statutory workers in her family and wasn't keen to involve the children in further interviews. She was, however, persuaded by the worker's argument that this would be the best way to begin to verify safety. Although the mother was not involved in the interviews she was very protective and monitored how the children reacted after the first session. The worker saw this as a positive sign of a mother concerned for her children, and this view was confirmed when, at subsequent interviews, the mother was quite relaxed about the involvement, once she had assured herself the children were comfortable.

At the first interview with the children they made it very clear they wanted the meetings with the worker over as quickly as possible. The worker negotiated with them and they agreed to three visits of 40 minutes each (she allowed the children to negotiate her down from 45 minutes). The worker felt that this was a small but important step in letting the children know they could influence what was happening. As it turned out each session lasted longer than 40 minutes, and it was the worker who had to let the children know that they had gone overtime.

In her contact with the family, more signs of safety became apparent to the worker. It was evident that there was a very good relationship between the mother and the children. There were clear demonstrations of spontaneous affection and the house had a very child-focused feel about it. The children were clearly thriving and were comfortable in their home. When interviewed, the children knew exactly why their father had been in jail, and they knew which children their father had "touched." Their mother had explained it all clearly to them. The worker also found that the children had an extensive network of adults (the majority of whom knew of the offenses), both in their family and outside, whom they readily identified as people they could tell if they felt threatened.

The only thing that concerned the worker a little was that the eldest child, when discussing adults he could trust, indicated that it would be a very bad thing if their family had to split up. The worker was somewhat concerned that perhaps the child would keep secrets because of fear of splitting the family. The children scaled safety on two scenarios, the first with their mother present and the second with only their father. The youngest scaled safety with the mother at 10, the eldest at 9. With their father, their ratings dropped to 3 and 5 respectively, though at the subsequent meeting the eldest stated that, on thinking about it, his view was that his safety would be a 7.

In this family, the mother was the exclusive caregiver of the children, and the children were never alone with their father, so the lower ratings did not concern the worker. So, in this context, the lower ratings, while of concern, did not create a practical safety issue for the worker. Further, the father's one complaint about his life was that his wife was "the boss" of the family, overseeing and directing all family arrangements. While this concerned the father, it meant the worker was even more confident of the children's safety. However, both the worker and the mother felt that the father's lack of involvement with the children needed to be addressed. Both the children and the father wanted to have more to do with each other, although the father had little idea how to begin such involvement. After discussions facilitated by the worker, over which she gave the mother a right of veto, it was agreed that the children would begin weekend sporting activities in which the father would be involved.

On the basis of the safety that she had discovered and consolidated, the worker was able to write a very clear and detailed report that recommended case closure.

The second case involved a blended family, made up of a mother and father, their two young children, and the mother's primary-school-aged children from a previous relationship. The man (we will refer to him as the stepfather in this example, since the concerns of the statutory agency related mainly to his nine-year-old step-daughter) had been jailed for the sexual abuse of a 10-year-old relative of the mother's.

On his release, the family wanted to reunite, but a condition of the stepfather's parole stipulated that he only have visitation rights and must reside outside the family home. At this point the parents had adopted a position of "us against the world," and they had no time for workers from the statutory agency. The statutory agency was very concerned about the situation. Their concern was heightened, since the relationship between mother and daughter was very poor, and it was uncertain how protective the mother would be toward the daughter. The mother continually expressed her dependence on her husband: she was almost completely financially dependent on him and suffered considerable health problems. She also perceived that she needed him to read to the children and help with their education, since she had significant reading problems due to her own learning difficulties. The stepfather was spending extended periods at the family home, and the statutory agency was concerned that he might be staying overnight.

The child protection worker and a support worker began to work with the family. The support worker particularly focused on getting to know the mother, learning about her day-to-day concerns, and assisting her practically. The worker sought the mother's cooperation to interview the daughter a number of times on a similar basis as described in the previous case. The worker was particularly concerned about the situation because the girl had no understanding of why her stepfather had been in jail, and the girl rated her sense of comfort and security in her family at a 4 out of 10.

At the same time, the worker got to know the mother, finding out how she experienced her life. The mother quickly made her position regarding the past events very clear. She felt that, while her partner might have been prosecuted, imprisoned, and forced to live outside of the family, it was she that carried the brunt of the punishment: The family now lived in poverty because her husband was unlikely to resume working until he was able to leave the metropolitan area. She was alienated from her family because she had chosen to stay with her husband even though he had abused a relative she cared for. She had had to take on all the family responsibilities, a particular burden to her since her health was so poor.

It was important to this woman that the worker understand the impact on her life due to the authorities' prosecution of her husband. The mother felt betrayed by the authorities since, although it was she who had disclosed the abuse, once her husband had been prosecuted, no one thought to offer support to her. She was not approached again by professionals until her husband was released from prison. It became apparent that much of the mother's "us against the world" attitude began to dissolve as the worker made sure the mother felt understood. This allowed other matters to be addressed. Slowly, and in small ways, the worker helped the mother to improve her relationship with her daughter. For example, the mother began to spend individual time with the daughter, which the child had clearly desired. The worker was careful to regularly compliment the mother for her efforts and how she had coped with the whole ordeal. As the worker built a relationship with both parents, it also became evident that they were dissatisfied with their marriage relationship.

The caseworker also began to talk with the parents about the fact that the daughter did not know why her stepfather had been jailed and that the stepfather had made no apology to the mother's family for what he had done. Utilizing the stepfather's desire to be allowed to go home and the mother's position that her husband needed to take some real responsibility to make things right, the worker got the man to prepare written drafts of an explanation for his stepdaughter and the apology to his wife's family. At the mother's initiative, an agreement was made that she would not assist her husband in these tasks, and the mother denied his requests even though he sought her help. After the worker had approved what he had written, the stepfather, with the worker present, explained to his stepdaughter why he had been in jail. He also made his apology to his wife's family. As with the mother, the worker made sure to give him support and compliments for his courage.

Following these developments, the daughter's rating of her security and (what could now be rated openly as her safety) increased to 8 out of 10. The girl was pleased that she now knew what had occurred, that she had more influence in the family, and that her relationship with her mother had improved. The worker was also pleased to identify a reliable adult friend of the family who the daughter would be able to talk to if she felt her safety was compromised.

As a result of all of this, the workers recommended to a joint child protection and parole case conference that the stepfather could return home. Interestingly, at this meeting the parents said they were not ready for the reunion. There were still unresolved issues, specifically concerning their relationship, and they were seeking counseling for this. This honesty and restraint on the part of the parents was a final sign of safety and led the statutory agency to close the case.

These two cases highlight, as have many cases studies throughout this book, that a purposive focus on goals and safety, allied with the creation of a working partnership between the family and worker, can bring very complicated child protection cases to constructive resolution.

CHAPTER NINE

Focusing on Good Practice: The Key to Successful Implementation

The signs of safety approach seeks to foster partnership between professionals and families, and there is considerable momentum throughout the child protection world to move in the same direction. What is frequently overlooked, however, is the careful consultation and training process that is required to equip workers to integrate and consistently deliver collaborative practice. It is one thing for policymakers and managers to call for partnership; it is another to implement it. The signs of safety approach has been developed in conjunction with almost 100 service delivery staff, and we believe we have learned a great deal over the past five years about successfully training child protection workers to engage with both the general principles of working in partnership and the signs of safety model more specifically. This chapter sets out to present some of what we have learned.

GOOD PRACTICE IN CHILD PROTECTION

As we observed earlier, practice in child protection has a propensity to become a problem-saturated and risk-dominated endeavor. Workers are often focused on the case that has just "blown up" or looks like it might, horror stories from the past abound, and supervision and case discussions frequently focus on the worst scenarios. This is a difficult environment in which to foster good practice and a healthy sense of competence in workers. In this regard, we sometimes use an analogy to sports. No successful sporting coach anywhere in the world would allow players on his/her team to focus excessively on their worst games, greatest failures, and worst fears and realistically expect a good performance. Sometimes it seems that this is exactly how professional child protection staff approach their work. Surprisingly though, we know from firsthand experience that even with the worst cases in the most overworked child protection agencies in the poorest of urban settings in the world, good child protection work is still being done.

Throughout this book, we have deliberately presented cases in which workers have purposefully built working partnerships with family members to increase the safety of the children involved. In our view, there is a great need for stories and examples of good practice in child protection to balance the negative and fear-laden tales that abound in the field. Stories of good practice offer ideas, direction, and inspiration for other workers (especially new workers) regarding what they can achieve and how to approach the work. Eliciting and amplifying examples of good practice is vital for enhancing morale and implementing any new approach, and it is certainly a central strategy for assisting workers to learn and implement the signs of safety approach.

It is our experience that child protection workers relish the opportunity to talk about aspirations, success, and possibilities for improvement within their work. This was further confirmed to us when we read of the Oregon experience (described more fully in chapter 1), where workers "lined up to participate" when asked to offer their best ideas for improving practice, ultimately generating the family unity meeting model (Graber, Keys, & White, 1996).

Good Practice Does Not Equal
Happy Endings

Before proceeding to the subject of fostering good practice, it is important to distinguish good practice from "happy endings." Good practice is professional endeavor that reflects the sorts of practice principles described in chapter 2. Examples of good practice could therefore include a worker "talking down" an angry and aggressive father, another who draws out a sullen child, a worker retaining an open mind until everyone involved has been able to have their say, a systematic and careful gathering of information regarding both danger and safety, and so on. Any or all of these may occur in any given case, even though the ultimate case outcome may be deemed ambivalent or even unsuccessful. It is our conviction, however, that good practice should still be identified and affirmed, all the more so because the child protection field is one where "happy endings" may be few and far between.

When training child protection workers, it is vital to approach them respectfully, remaining cognizant of the skills and experience they already draw upon. One of the real privileges we have found in our child protection work is to hear of the skillful practice that statutory workers can undertake given the right training and consultation process. Child protection workers grapple daily with the realities of one of the hardest roles in the helping professions and quickly become alienated if they are approached as if the trainer, consultant, or supervisor has all the answers or will supplant their existing practice.

Much of what we will describe in this chapter is about eliciting, amplifying, and celebrating good child protection practice as a primary vehicle for energizing and motivating workers to engage with the approach. We attempt to train and consult with workers in the same way we ask them to interact with the families they see; therefore we:

- Assume good practice already exists and work carefully to elicit this.
- Define as clearly as we can what we want the workers to do.
- Compliment successful implementation.

Not surprisingly, workers readily engage with a training and consultation process that focuses on good practice, because they are being affirmed for work they already do. Linking existing good practice with the new skills, thinking, and practice being called for energizes the learning process and is a practical way of creating change from the ground up.

TRAINING WORKERS IN THE SIGNS OF SAFETY APPROACH

Paulo Freire (1972) describes what he calls the "banking model" of education whereby the expert teacher deposits information into the student. Although most of us, if we thought about it, would repudiate such a model of education, professional training often takes on this feel. It is alienating to participants and will most often result in the material presented being shelved in its training folder and having little impact on practice. The signs of safety approach to child protection aspires to partnership, and since we want to see professional practice with service recipients and with other professionals conducted collaboratively, we consider it vital that the approach is presented and trained in a manner that builds partnership between trainer and the worker/trainees as well as between the participants themselves.

The Signs of Safety Training
Program Format

Our full training program incorporates five days of training over four weeks. The first two days are essentially focused on solution-focused brief therapy, particularly as it is applied to typical "multi-problem child welfare" casework. These first two days offer a grounding in the thinking and techniques that underpin the signs of safety approach, since this model has arisen out of the pragmatically change-oriented brief therapy approach to problems and their resolution.

The second two days of training, two weeks later, focus specifically on the signs of safety approach. We explore the purpose of the model, which is to foster skillful and considered use of professional authority while creating a cooperative and purposive worker-family relationship focused on safety for the child(ren). We consider the nature of good child protection practice from the perspective of the service recipients and professional, similar to the material described in chapter 1. Following this, we present the practice elements and, as we have described, consider their use in the current practice of the participants. Then we begin the process—usually through role play—of exploring how the elements might be applied from intake through to assessment, as this book does in chapters 3 through to 7.

Throughout this participatory training process, we intersperse case presentations by workers experienced in the signs of safety approach. Often this is videotaped material of workers describing their own successful implementation during previous training and consultation programs. We also offer copies of numerous completed assessments like those throughout the book. We invite a child protection worker who has experience using the approach to come and talk directly to the trainees. We know from regular feedback that the direct experience and case examples of colleagues make an enormous difference to trainees.

The fifth day's training, a further two weeks later, is set aside for workers to come back and report on their successes in imple-

TABLE 9.1
Outline of Five-Day Signs of Safety Training Program.

Days one and two: Applying solution-focused brief therapy to child welfare casework.

• Exploration of what participants want from training using scaling question exercise.
• History and development of brief therapy underlining its pragmatic emphasis on doing the least necessary to create requisite change.
• Exploration of principles that inform participant's professional practice, leading into presentation and discussion of principles behind solution-focused brief therapy.
• Presentation of solution-focused skills:

—Exception questions
—Goal-focused questions
—Scaling questions
—Interviewing techniques to elicit and amplify detail
—Compliments
—Tasks and interventions

• Training is illustrated with videotaped case material, and skill-building exercises are used throughout. The application of solution-focused brief therapy from commencement to closure is explored sequentially over the two days.

Days three and four: The signs of safety approach to child protection.

• Exploration of how participants have utilized first two days' training.
• What is good child protection practice: practitioner's views and service recipient's views.
• Partnership in child protection: a global perspective.
• Signs of safety practice principles.
• Overview of signs of safety practice elements. Training exercise: how do participants already utilize the practice elements in their work.
• Detailed presentation of practice elements with associated skill-building exercises following one case scenario through intake, investigation, and planning stages.
• Signs of safety assessment process is presented and practiced with several case scenarios.
• Several workers experienced in using the signs of safety approach present and discuss their casework.
• Exercise to prepare participants to use the approach with existing cases.

TABLE 9.1
Continued

Day five: Participants' use of the signs of safety approach: Successes and difficulties.

- Participants in turn describe successful use of the approach; participants' practice is amplified in detail by trainers.
- Case consultation with difficult cases. Participants develop signs of safety strategies for each case under consideration prior to any trainer input.
- Preparation for follow-up consultation (if this is to occur).
- Evaluation.

---

menting the model (in whole or in part) and to raise their general concerns and specific case issues. It cannot be emphasized enough that it is vital to always begin this day by first getting workers to describe their successes in detail. Only after every participant has had an opportunity to do this do we move onto concerns, difficulties, and questions. We have learned the hard way that if we operate in reverse order, beginning with the difficulties or questions of the group, we will rarely get to talk about good practice and successes.

Focusing on Success First

Wherever possible, we attempt to involve ourselves in three- to six-month follow-up projects during which we meet with the trainees once a month for a half-day consultation, and we also make ourselves available for phone consultation at any time during the project's life. The structure of the half-day follow-up sessions is identical to the fifth day's training: half the time is spent looking at successes and the other half at participants' concerns, difficulties, and questions. The successes always come first.

Approaching Workers as Competent Professionals

A good metaphor for the creation of partnership between trainers and participants is to think of the training process as carefully grafting new material onto a healthy plant. When we present the ideas and practice elements of the signs of safety, we are always looking for a "fit" with the existing aspirations and practice of those we are training. We frequently ask trainees to think of the best child protection worker they have ever encountered and to write down three attributes and skills of that worker that most characterize good practice. This tells us what the participants aspire to in their work. Having undertaken this exercise with many child protection workers in three different countries, we know that workers consistently aspire to collaborative practice. Thoburn et al. (1995) found the same result in their more systematic study of partnership in child protection. In this way we start from common ground; the worker's aspirations correlate with what we consider good practice and what consumers are looking for. In this way we begin to explore the thinking behind the signs of safety.

We pursue a similar training strategy when we outline the practice elements. We succinctly present short case vignettes to explain each element without going into detail. Once the trainees understand the elements, we break them into small groups of two or three to discuss examples in which they have already used one of these practice elements. We then invite the workers to describe their successes to the larger group. At such times we have heard about:

- A worker who took seriously a woman whose goal was to have her child returned to her, even though the child had already been adopted.
- Another who assisted a mother to get away from a violent relationship and into a new location and house.
- The story of a young mother with whom others had "failed," but the worker was able to build a relationship because she drew on and acknowledged the resource of the woman's poetry.
- A worker who was able to make some progress with an aggressive man when he observed that the man didn't always get angry with his children when he easily could have.
- Another worker who fostered a significant shift in a case because he listened to the parents' complaints that the "welfare" refused to acknowledge or do anything about their ideas.

Our experience tells us that the practice elements of the signs of safety are not new concepts and some workers are already doing these sorts of things some of the time. Workers who have completed our training tell us that, while the elements themselves may not be new, what is new for them is the structure that makes the material significant and meaningful in their interactions with families and in the assessment and planning processes.

The point is not to approach child protection workers as if the presenter is the repository of new and radical information that will completely transform their practice. This will only alienate child protection professionals who know the realities and difficulties they face daily. To enable them to engage with the signs of safety approach (or any other sort of model) success will be more likely when we approach workers and train them as competent professionals already carrying out good practice. Therefore, we keep this dynamic between presenting material and inviting descriptions of how they are already doing it, or would see themselves doing so as an ongoing process throughout training.

Case example

The process of focusing on successful implementation as the first item of business can have interesting results. For example, a worker* participating in a follow-up consultation made it clear that she was anxious to discuss ways to deal with clients who were difficult to engage because they were angrily stuck in their own opinions of a situation. The worker made it clear she wanted to focus on this immediately. As consultants, we held true to our commitment to discuss successes first. We let the worker know we would return to her concern immediately afterward.

The worker had recently commenced involvement with a mother and her 13-year-old son. The boy had a long history of being shunted back and forth across the country between the mother in one state and the father in another, following incidents of rebelliousness, truancy, and small offenses such as graffiti and shoplifting. The mother refused to have the child in her house again and demanded that "the welfare" take over his care because he was ruining her life and family. The boy had been in institutional care for over a month, and the statutory agency was placing considerable pressure on the woman to take him back into her care. The worker was instructed by her manager to persuade the mother to accept this course of action. At their first meeting the woman talked at the worker almost nonstop for over 40 minutes and made it quite clear that she refused to participate in any of "this social worker crap" to attempt to reunite her with her son.

When the worker told us how she had responded to the mother (in a moment we will look at the details of the worker's efforts), it became evident that she had worked very carefully and successfully

_____

*Vania Dapaz

in a difficult, problematic situation. By beginning with her success, we found that she was able to describe not only her own manner of implementing the signs of safety approach but also her own way of dealing with a client who was angry and talked nonstop. Elaboration on her success in this situation answered her own questions. If we had become engaged in describing what we thought should be done about such a case, we would have been much less helpful than was the process of the worker recognizing her own success. In these sessions it is common for participants to become aware of their own skillfulness as well as to answer each other's questions and problems. As consultants, our expertise is not so much in having the answers or giving direction but in facilitating conversations and descriptions that are sufficiently rich in detail as to be educative of what good practice looks like.

In this sort of consultation process we are also learning all the time. In fact, it is this process of action and reflection over successive joint work projects that has refined and evolved the signs of safety model. When we first designed the approach, we were very focused on how the elements might be structured in interviews, what questions might best be used and so on. We soon learned from experience that this formulaic focus on our part paled in comparison to the creative ways workers themselves found to build partnerships and implement the model. This exploration and discovery of how workers implement the approach is far more important than any aggrandizement of our own expertise and ideas and consistently energizes and inspires both the child protection workers and ourselves to continue to experiment with the model.

AMPLIFYING *HOW* IT WAS DONE

In an environment where they feel safe and valued for their contribution, child protection workers will relish the experience of telling their stories of good practice. On one occasion, we were facilitating a follow-up session with almost a dozen workers and, after the first three or four had offered their examples of good practice, we noticed that one of the workers who had not yet spoken, was crying quietly. We wondered if the details of one of the cases had adversely affected her, though we doubted this, since the woman was a child protection worker with many years' experience. When it came time for this woman to relate her story of success, we asked her if she was willing to tell us what it was that caused her to cry. She had no trouble in relating that this was the first time in her 13 years of experience that she could remember having any sort of focused discussion on good child protection practice.

Frequently, though, stories of good practice are just that: stories. Though these stories are inspiring, they are not necessarily instructive for other participants in replicating the good practice. It can even become problematic if success stories are too generalized, because some participants will find themselves feeling, "I couldn't do that." Thus, it is the facilitator's role to elicit the sort of detail that exemplifies *how* the success was achieved.

Two case examples

To demonstrate the manner in which the consultant can elicit and amplify success, we will consider part of the dialogue involved in the case of the mother who had rejected her son.

ANDREW So what made the difference? How did you get the mom to stop talking at you and start talking with you?

WORKER I asked her why the boy had come back to Western Australia, and she said that the ex (husband) had said that if she didn't take the boy back he was going to a welfare home and "no mother wants her child in a welfare home." So I said, "Hang on a moment, that's where he is now!" (It had not occurred to the mother that, by placing her son in residential care, she had done exactly what she believed her ex-husband should not do.) She was stunned, was absolutely agog. So this was a moment for me to actually say something. I could actually get a word in because she was so stunned by that. . . .

At the same time, there was all this pressure to get the kid out of the residential unit and get him back to his mom. I tried to resist this pressure, because part of me felt it was unrealistic. It was an unrealistic objective at the moment.

ANDREW *(speaking to broader group)* And isn't that a lovely story about just coming down to a small change? You set the small goal of building any connection with the mother so she will begin to talk to you. You found that chink of light about the dad wanting to put him in the welfare home. How did you move on from there?

WORKER   Well, I realized that she thought I hadn't heard her position so I fed it back to her. I told her I understood that she thought he was a danger to her current family, and I said, "Obviously, your new family is really, really important to you." Then she went off on that tangent and starting to talking about her new husband and the kids and saying, "Yes, they are very important to me." She had the little boy with her in the office and he started doing something, and the way she handled him was really nice—he started making a lot of noise and she was very patient, and I complimented her on the way that she handled him.

ANDREW   You see *(talking again to the rest of the group)* another piece, she [the worker] discovered new components that helped build some difference with this woman. I bet there was a whole slew of other pieces that we haven't heard about. You didn't just go from there to there *(from the woman's monologue to a dialogue)*. She had to be heard. You thought about what she wanted, which was the new family. You responded by complimenting her about the boy. This is the sort of stuff that gets the dialogue going.

WORKER   That's right. Because we had been going in with the hard line about responsibility and it was just getting nowhere. That was frustrating and I felt myself getting annoyed with her, you know, like, "How dare you do this to a thirteen-year-old boy? His behavior is not that of a psychopath. It's that of a rejected child." Then I had to stop and think "Okay, this is going nowhere. There is no point to getting annoyed, just go with the flow a bit more."

ANDREW   So you created some headspace for yourself as well.

WORKER   And took a step back from other people's agendas too, like the pressure that came from the senior case supervisor.

The upshot of this interview was that the worker was able to get the mother to consider how the boy might be feeling. As a result, the mother made a commitment to start phoning her son at the residential unit in which he was staying. No happy endings were in sight in this case, and as far as we know none occurred. However, that does not take away in the slightest from the careful and very good work involved in engaging the mother. One of the reasons the worker was so concerned about how to engage someone who was angry and opinionated was that, under the imperative of trying to reunite the boy with his mother (at which she felt she was not succeeding), she had failed to notice what she had already achieved.

To arrive at the sort of detail that is described here, the facilitator will frequently have to question the worker carefully. The questioning revealed the worker's compliment about the mother's parenting, and her focus on the mother's goal of wanting a good family life. It was also important for the other participants to realize that the worker had given the woman considerable time to speak and then let her know that she understood her position of not wanting her teenage son living with her. All these interactions set the context for the worker to initiate a genuine dialogue. We also underlined the importance of setting an achievable goal and holding the supervisor's expectations in abeyance.

Eliciting this sort of detail requires discipline and careful focus on the part of the consultant or supervisor. Certain approaches need to be avoided. In a case description of this sort it is easy to get drawn into a discussion of what should be done next. If this transpires, the facilitator will find many other participants quickly joining the discussion, and the focus on the successful application of the signs of safety approach will be difficult to re-establish. If the worker wishes to discuss what to do next, we hold that discussion after all participants have had a turn presenting their experiences of successfully utilizing some part of the model.

Sometimes, workers describe a case from commencement to closure. The worker* in this case is sensitive to describing how the good practice was achieved and, in her own description of the casework, provides considerable detail as to how she collaborated with the mother and daughter involved.

WORKER   I managed to use it (the signs of safety approach) on a case that went from beginning to end, which I found quite interesting because it ended up quite differently from what you'd expect. I had a child who had been quite seriously physically abused and was placed in foster care. When I spoke to the mom she basically told me

---

*Andrea Nixon

to "bugger off" and said she didn't want her child back, we could place her wherever we liked.

Normally I would have probably said, "Hang on a minute," but I thought, "Well, that's where she is and that's what she wants, so let's leave it at that." I said to her, "Okay, if that's what you want, that's what we'll do," and I talked with her about where her daughter could go and various placement options. Then I talked to the girl and said, "What do you want to do?" She said, "I don't want to go home." So I said, "Fine," and I talked with her about where she wanted to go.

I looked into alternative placements for this child. Eventually, after a couple of weeks, mom called me back and said, "I think I'd like to talk a bit more about this." So we talked and I said, "Well, I've looked into this and that and we can place her here or there," and she said, "Well, you know, things aren't usually this bad. It was really a one-time thing." She was more willing to talk and I said, "The girl's still saying she doesn't want to come home, so we'll just keep going the way we're going and see what happens."

I left it for another week and the mom called me up again and said, "I'll do whatever you want, I'll do whatever you want," and I said, "I haven't asked you to do anything yet." *(Everyone laughs)*.

ANDREW Hang on a minute, have you been reading Milton Erickson? The way you've utilized the mother's and daughter's position sure seems like it *(more laughter)*.

WORKER Well I said, "Okay, we'll get the two of you together and we'll chat about it." So I got them both in and we talked about what had happened, what brought it on, and what we could do about it to stop it from happening again. The girl said, "I want to go home," and mom said, "I want her home," and I said, "Fine. Go home." Normally, I wouldn't have handled it that way. It was an interesting process, and I actually felt really comfortable about the girl going home, despite the fact that it was quite serious abuse and I would not have felt happy before. In fact, the Police Child Abuse Unit wasn't happy about it at all, but there were different perceptions. I mean, they saw the woman once, when she told them

to "shove it." Of course their perception of her was
different from mine.

When I wrote it up, I went through all the headings
(of the practice elements) of all the signs of safety stuff
and we discussed all of them. I probably didn't do it
strictly in the correct way, but we had discussed exceptions and we'd discussed how confident they felt about
maintaining the changes and how confident they were
to do something about it and we talked about life generally and scaling. We had discussed it all. When I went
to write it up, I could write the assessment up under
those headings, and it actually looked pretty good. I
mean, it actually made a lot of sense in terms of why
I'd sent the kid home. I think we do those things without
consciously being aware of it. But when you actually
consciously think about writing it up that way, it makes
a lot of sense.

ANDREW   What were the things in there that gave you enough
confidence that there was enough safety for this kid to
go home?

WORKER   Both of them said that this was a rarity, that normally
life was okay and that this was basically just an exception
to the rule. They talked about their feelings for each
other and they obviously had quite a lot of regard for
each other. They told me that the abuse had been
brought on by a fairly minor thing and it had just escalated out of control. Besides, the girl had handled it very
well. She had known who to call, who to approach, and
how to get assistance, so I was confident that if it did
ever happen again, she would know what to do. We
talked about that, and about protective behavior. They
also agreed to undertake some counseling, so I felt pretty
good about that.

ANDREW   How was that different from what you would have done
before?

WORKER   I think I normally would have not allowed this kid to
go home because it was serious abuse. I would have
looked at us taking some statutory action down the road,
but I didn't even talk about that. We just talked about
her staying in care, maybe going to stay with someone
else later on. It was nebulous, but I never actually men-

tioned taking statutory action. I acted more on what the girl wanted than what the department wanted.

ANDREW So you knew what the department wanted, but you didn't say that to the mom.

WORKER Yes, I didn't say that to the mom because she was pretty oppositional anyway, so I talked about the child's perspective: She was frightened to come home, she didn't want to come home, and why. I was very up-front with the mom about what the girl said, which upset her a bit, but I think since it was the girl's perspective rather than mine, it made a big difference.

So, I was very honest with them—not that I'm not honest normally—I just think that I handled it differently. I don't think I once said, "We think you should do this or that," which I probably would have done before. It was more a matter of going with the flow.

ANDREW You didn't set it up as though it was the department against the mom. You could just say, "Well, she doesn't want to come home, and that's it." You utilized the mom's position. You seemed to leave it more between them, like the mother had to win the girl over, and allowed what they wanted to evolve over time.

WORKER And the other thing that I didn't do, which I could have done, was discuss it with anyone. Normally I'd have talked about it with a senior caseworker or someone with experience and said, "Look, I've got this case, and this is what I'm doing. What do you think?" This time I thought, "No, no, I'll just see what happens." So, when we reached this decision, I went to see the senior casework supervisor and said, "I'm sending this kid home. It was fairly serious abuse, but I think she'll be okay." I presented my assessment, and the supervisor accepted it.

ANDREW Will there be monitoring or follow-up?

WORKER There will be some through the school, but the agency will not be involved. In the past we probably would have been, but when I did the write-up with all those headings, it was clear that we had no role. There was nothing we could do other than sit on the sidelines and watch, which seems a bit pointless.

Relating examples of good practice within a group of peers is a powerful learning tool. Everyone seems to enjoy celebrating good work, and the number of times laughter intersperses these examples always gives us the sense that we must be doing something right. It's easy to identify outstanding aspects of each example. So, following the case presentation described above, we asked the group, "What did you think was most important about how this case was handled?" We invited group members to overtly make their own judgments about how good practice occurs.

The consensus in the group (and among subsequent trainees to whom we have shown this example on videotape) was that the worker seemed have faith in the mother and daughter, so she allowed time for them to come to their own resolution, rather than driving the agency's agenda. Additionally, she took them seriously instead of fighting with them or trying to persuade them from their particular positions. She paid careful attention to their ideas.

In focusing on the successful implementation of the signs of safety approach, we attempt to find as many feedback loops as possible for workers to reflect on the good practice they describe. To this end, as we have just intimated, we videotape worker's descriptions of their successful practice and often transcribe what they tell us. The workers can review their own and each other's descriptions, and, if they wish, they can show the videos and the transcripts to other colleagues. This is particularly useful since participants are often asked by their colleagues at their office or agency to present what they have learned. Workers take a lot of pride in using these examples of good signs of safety practice, and this reinforces their ability to successfully implement the approach.

WHY GOOD CHILD PROTECTION
PRACTICE CAN GO UNDERGROUND

As we train more child protection workers and gain more experience in eliciting and amplifying good practice it becomes clear that child protection workers have a propensity to keep their achievements to themselves.

Talking about successful practice often flies in the face of the culture of agencies that focus on the difficulties and problems of the work. Most of us are loath to blow our own trumpet in front of our colleagues, so it is easier to talk about failures and concerns than successes.

There can also be structural impediments to making good child protection practice public. Furthermore, as the worker in the case we have just considered stated, "The other thing that I didn't do, which I could have done, was discuss it with anyone." This worker knew that what she was doing was not normal practice within her agency. The normal practice would have been to put greater pressure on the mother to face the issues.

All statutory agencies have standardized procedures and protocols as well as a more generalized culture of how business is done. Numerous commentators, for example, Sharland, Jones, Aldgate, Seal, and Croucher (1995) and Jeffreys and Stevenson (1997), have observed that these protocols and norms can hinder the worker in developing plans that are based on the particularities of the case in hand.

Workers pursuing collaborative strategies often operate at the periphery of the protocols and conventions of normal agency practice because they feel that following the standard agency line is likely to alienate the client. Parents articulate the same dilemma in a more down-to-earth fashion when they receive services they perceive to be focused on protocol. Almost every consumer study we have looked at finds some service recipients commenting, "The worker was only really interested in doing it by the book!"

Managers and policymakers calling for collaborative practice must develop protocols that standardize and contribute to safe practice but also allow for flexibility in the interaction between workers and families. In some places in the world (for example, in New Zealand) a case consultation service, which is outside the supervisory and management hierarchy, is provided to workers so they can speak frankly about their practice (and for other reasons). As trainers and consultants we are more likely to hear about good practice, since we are completely external to the agencies involved. However, we have met many experienced workers who have developed their own unique ways of addressing agency requirements while also delivering a client-sensitive service, often by collaborating and discussing case practice with trusted colleagues. As Jeffreys and Stevenson observe, "Competent and experienced workers learn there is usually room to interpret standardized procedures, rather than be dominated by them" (1997, p. 38).

Good Practice Needs Broad Support: Some Thoughts on Intra- and Interagency Collaboration

There are many elements involved in creating good child protection practice. It requires good training for field staff, thoughtful supervision and management, and communication and collaboration among all levels of the agency. Management must be seen as mindful of casework issues and supportive of field staff. There needs to be collaboration and partnership between those public officials who set the agendas for the statutory agency, those in management, and those in the field. Optimal child protection practice does not end within the bounds of the statutory agency. There also needs to be a good relationship between the statutory agency and other professional child protection services (hospitals, schools, police, welfare agencies, other providers of treatment services, etc.). The better the relationship between the statutory agency and the broader community, the better the service it can deliver.

Conversely, when officials are perceived to be motivated by such things as winning popularity or pursuing efficiency and economic imperatives, managers are seen to be removed from the experience and needs of field staff, field staff feel overloaded, other professionals in secondary child protection agencies are critical or even acrimonious toward the statutory agency, tertiary schools of social work are antagonistic about child protection work, or the broader community is fearful of social workers that might take their children and attempt to control their lives, children are placed at greater risk of maltreatment. Sadly, these negative characteristics are frequently used to describe our child protection systems in many parts of the world. Both perceived and real antagonisms between different players in the child protection process allow children to fall through the cracks.

The notion of partnership advocated throughout this book is as applicable to the relationship between the parents/family and the worker as it is to any relationship in the child protection process. The child's safety is best served by collaboration, respect, and cooperation among all parties concerned with child protection. This reflects the old, frequently cited adage, "It takes a village to raise a child." The notion of partnership and collaboration needs to inform the whole context of child protection and relationships between professionals and families, organizations, and other professionals.

We are regularly involved in providing training to child protection professionals. Sometimes we train in mixed settings (a mix of statutory officers, health and hospital professionals, residential and alternative care workers, and so on), at other times within a single agency or service. Whatever the setting, it is not uncommon to find one group being critical of others. For example, residential care workers might be critical of the perceived heavy-handedness of the statutory professionals, and statutory workers may be critical of health professionals for not paying enough attention to visible risk factors.

The culture of a particular agency or service can evolve in such a way that the professionals within that service are continually talking to each other as if "we" know best and others are always letting "us" down. This does not foster good practice. In fact it can be downright dangerous if different professionals involved with the same family alienate themselves from one another, sending the family mixed messages and compromising children's safety. The case example involving the rural doctor and statutory agency (presented in chapter 4) exemplifies this. As we observed in that chapter if a permanent breakdown in the relationship between the medical practitioner and the agency had occurred, children in the small town and surrounding areas would have been less safe.

When a single agency shows antagonism toward other groups of child protection professionals, we will often bring the training to a halt and address the issue. We might ask the group to scale as a percentage how often they believe their agency delivers good practice in its child protection services and then to provide a judgment regarding how often the agency that is being criticized does so. Inevitably, the latter receives a lower score (sometimes significantly). We may ask if anyone feels concerned about the judgments they are passing on their colleagues, and sometimes a courageous individual will raise a concern. If none are raised we will raise our own concerns, namely that these negative stories undermine the possibility of interagency collaboration with a vital player in the child protection process. Then we invite someone to describe an experience of successful collaboration between themselves and workers from the agency under attack. Inevitably, these stories are not very difficult to find, it is simply that a culture of complaint and critique can be very persuasive, and, in this environment, collaboration is normally not highlighted or affirmed.

Good practice in child protection requires cooperation and respect between all the professionals involved. Training professionals from different settings in signs of safety often gives us the opportunity to enhance such collaboration. Where we can elicit stories of good practice from professionals working in the different agencies, all participants gain more insight into the roles of their colleagues. Inevitably, agencies become more understanding and are often surprised by others' competency. This is one way in which a focus on good practice can advance collaboration between agencies.

Increasing Child Protection Workers' Sense of Self-Respect and Competence

In our training and consultation work, we always survey participants to gauge their assessment of the impact and value of the sessions. Workers consistently tell us that our positive approach to them and their practice, as well as the training and the signs of safety model help them value their work. Recently, we decided to more closely assess this aspect of what the workers were telling us.

We asked one group of 15 workers to give a 0–10 rating regarding their own expertise and skillfulness before and after the signs of safety training process. On average, the group increased the rating of their own practice and role by almost a full point. The result is not startling, but for us the improvement was based on:

- Communicating our respect for and encouragement of the child protection work they undertake.
- Offering them a model that presents positive and specific direction to their practice and encourages them to view the families they work with as potential partners.
- Working with them in a manner whereby we elicit and affirm good practice.

Much is written and described about the low morale of workers in the child protection field. Therefore, it is of considerable satisfaction to us that we can collaborate with child protection workers in a way that makes them feel a little better about their professional role and how they see themselves undertaking it.

Final Word

We hope the reader has received the message throughout this book that the signs of safety is a dynamic approach that has evolved through our collaboration with many child protection workers and other colleagues. The creation of the signs of safety model resulted from the question we asked each other: How could the ideas and thinking of brief therapy apply to child protection casework? We have learned that there is no final answer to this question.

As we stated in the previous chapter, each time a child protection worker applies our model in the field and then describes his or her endeavors to us, we learn more about applying the approach. It should be clear to the reader that there is no right way to apply the approach. Every time a worker applies the model to a child protection case, it evolves. We will have succeeded in this book if the reader finds enough inspiration in what we have written to utilize some of our ideas and strategies in their own practice. Wherever this occurs, the signs of safety model will continue to evolve, as will the endeavor of finding creative ways to build partnerships between workers and families in the emotionally charged environment of child protection.

References

Ban, P. (1992). Client participation—Beyond the rhetoric. *Children Australia, 17(4)*, 16–20.

Ban, P. (1993). Family decision making—The model as practiced in New Zealand and its relevance in Australia. *Australian Social Work 46(3)*, 22–30.

Bentovim, A., Elton, A., & Tranter, M. (1987). Prognosis for rehabilitation after abuse. *Adoption and Fostering, 11(1)*, 26–31.

Berg, I.K. (1994). *Family based service: A solution-focused approach.* New York: Norton.

Berg, I.K., & de Shazer, S. (1993). Making numbers talk: Language in therapy. In S. Friedman (Ed.), *The new language of change: Constructive collaboration in psychotherapy.* New York: Guilford.

Berg, I.K., & Kelly, S. (in press). *Building solutions in child protective services.* New York: Norton.

Besarov, D. (1985). "Doing something" about child abuse: The need to narrow the grounds for state intervention. *Harvard Journal of Law and Public Policy, 8*, 539–589.

Besarov, D. (1990). Gaining control over child abuse reports. *Public Welfare, 48(2)*, 34–39.

Birchall, E., & Hallett, C. (1995). *Working together in child protection.* London: HMSO.

Boscolo, L., Cecchin, G., Hoffman, L., & Penn, P. (1987). *Milan systemic family therapy.* New York: Basic Books.

Briere, J.N. (1992). *Child abuse and trauma. Theory and treatment of the lasting effects.* Newbury Park: Sage.

Brown, C. (1986). *Child abuse parents speaking: Parents' impressions of social workers and the social work process.* School for Advanced Urban Studies, University of Bristol.

Buchanan, A. (1996). *Cycles of child maltreatment. Facts, fallacies and interventions.* Chichester: Wiley.

203

Cade, B., & O'Hanlon, W. (1993). *A brief guide to brief therapy*. New York: Norton.

Calder, (1995). Child protection: Balancing paternalism and partnership. *British Journal of Social Work, 25(6)*, 749–766.

Cleaver, H., & Freeman, P. (1995). *Parental perspectives in cases of suspected child abuse*. London: HSMO.

Corby, C. (1987). *Working with child abuse: Social work practice and the child abuse system*. Milton Keynes: Open University Press.

Dale, P., Davies, M., Morrison, T., & Waters, J. (1986). *Dangerous families: Assessment and treatment of child abuse*. London: Routledge.

Dartington Social Research Unit. (1995). *Child protection messages from research*. London: HSMO.

Deal, R., & Veeken, J. (1996). *Scales, tools for change*. Bendigo: St. Lukes.

Dean, G., & Locke, M. (1983). The creation of therapeutic realities in initial child protection interventions. *Australian Journal of Family Therapy, 4(2)*, 91–98.

DeJong, P., & Berg, I.K. (1998). *Interviewing for solutions*. Pacific Grove, CA: Brooks/Cole.

de Shazer, S. (1984). The death of resistance. *Family Process, 2*, 79–93.

de Shazer, S. (1985). *Keys to solution in brief therapy*. New York: Norton.

de Shazer, S. (1988). *Clues: Investigating solutions in brief therapy*. New York: Norton.

de Shazer, S. (1991). *Putting difference to work*. New York: Norton.

de Shazer, S., Berg, I.K., Lipchik, E., Nunnally, E., Molnar, A., Gingerich, W.C., & Weiner-Davis, M. (1986). Brief therapy: Focused solution development. *Family Process, 25*, 207–221.

de Shazer, S., & Berg, I.K. (1995). The brief therapy tradition. In J. Weakland & W. Ray (Eds.), *Propagations: Thirty years of influence from the Mental Research Institute*. New York: Haworth Press.

Dingwall, R., Eekelaar, J., & Murray, T. (1983). *The protection of children; State intervention and family life*. Oxford: Blackwell.

Dolan, Y. (1998). *One small step*. Watsonville, CA: Papier-Mache Press.

Doueck, H.J., Levine, M., & Bronson, D.E. (1993). Risk assessment in child protection services. An evaluation of the child at risk field system. *Journal of Interpersonal Violence, 8(4)*, 446–457.

Doyle, C. (1997). Emotional abuse of children: Issues for intervention. *Child Abuse Review, 6*, 330–342.

Edwards, S. (1991). *The application of single-subject research methodology in a public welfare agency*. Unpublished Social Work Honors Thesis, University of Western Australia: Perth.

Edwards, S., & Turnell, A. (1995). *Signs of safety, a workbook: Applying solution-focused procedure and ideas to child protection casework*. Perth: CBTS Publications.

English, D. J., & Pecora, P. J. (1994). Risk assessment as a practice method in child protective services. *Child Welfare, 82(5)*, 451–473.

Essex, S., Gumbleton, J., & Luger, C. (1996). Resolutions: Working with families where responsibility for abuse is denied. *Child Abuse Review, 5,* 191–201.

Essex, S., & Gumbleton, J. (1999). Conversations in the "similar but different": Working with denial in cases of severe child abuse. *Australia and New Zealand Journal of Family Therapy.*

Fadiman, A. (1997). *The spirit catches you and you fall down.* New York: Farran, Straus, & Giroux.

Farmer, E. (1993). The impact of child protection interventions: The experiences of parents and children. In Lorraine Waterhouse (Ed.), *Child abuse and child abusers: Protection and prevention, research highlights in social work,* No. 24. London: Jessica Kingsley.

Farmer, E., & Owen, M. (1995). *Child protection practice: Private risks and public remedies.* London: HSMO.

Farmer, E., & Pollock, S. (1998). *Substitute care for sexually abused and abusing children.* Chichester: Wiley.

Farrow, F. (1996). *Child protection: Building community partnerships.* John F. Kennedy School of Government, Harvard University.

Finkelhor, D. (1990). Is child abuse overreported? *Public Welfare, 48(1),* 23–29.

Fisch, R. (1988). Training in the brief therapy model. In H. Liddle, D. Breunlin, & R. Schwartz (Eds.), *Handbook of family therapy training and supervision.* New York: Guilford.

Fisch, R., Weakland, J., & Segal, L. (1982). *Tactics of change.* San Francisco: Jossey-Bass.

Fitzpatrick, C., & Lang, M. (1996, January 18). Murder boy plea ignored: Family. *The West Australian,* p. 1.

Fleming, J. (1998). Valuing families in statutory practice. *Child Abuse Prevention, 6(1),* 1–4.

Freire, P. (1972). *Pedagogy of the oppressed.* Harmondsworth: Penguin Books.

Fryer, G.E., Bross, D.C., Krugman, R.D., Denson, D.B., & Baird, D. (1990). Good news for CPS workers. *Public Welfare, 48(1),* 38–41.

Furlong, M. (1989). Can a family therapist do statutory work? *Australian and New Zealand Journal of Family Therapy, 10(4),* 211–218.

Garbarino, J. (1977). The human ecology of child mistreatment. *Journal of Marriage and the Family, 39(4),* 721–735.

Gelles, R. (in press). Untreatable families. In R.M. Reece (Ed.), *The treatment of child abuse.* Baltimore: Johns Hopkins University Press.

Giardino, A.P., Christian, C.W., & Giardino, E.R. (1997). *A practical guide to the evaluation of child physical abuse and neglect.* Thousand Oaks, CA: Sage.

Gil, D.G. (1970). *Violence against children: Physical abuse in the United States.* Cambridge, MA: Harvard University Press.

Giovannoni, J.M., & Becerra, R.M. (1979). *Defining child abuse.* New York: Free Press.

Graber, L., Keys, T., & White, J. (1996). Family group decision-making in the United States: The case of Oregon. In J. Hudson, A. Morris, G. Maxwell, & B. Galaway (Eds.), *Family group conferences*. Monsey: Willow Tree Press.

Haley, J. (1980). *Leaving home: The therapy of disturbed young people*. New York: McGraw-Hill.

Hallett, C., & Birchall, E. (1992). *Coordination and child protection*. Edinburgh: HSMO.

Hallett, C. (1995). *Interagency coordination in child protection*. London: HMSO.

Hassall, I. (1996). Origin and development of family group conferences. In J. Hudson, A. Morris, G. Maxwell, & B. Galaway (Eds.), *Family group conferences*. Monsey: Willow Tree Press.

Hopwood, L., & de Shazer, S. (1994). From here to who knows where: The continuing evolution of solution-focused brief therapy. In M. Elkaim (Ed.), *Therapies familiales: Les approches pricipaux*. Paris: Editiones du Seuil.

Hudson, J., Morris, A., Maxwell, G., & Galaway, B. (1996). Introduction. In J. Hudson, A. Morris, G. Maxwell, & B. Galaway (Eds.), *Family group conferences*. Monsey: Willow Tree Press.

Hudson, J., Morris, A., Maxwell, G., & Galaway, B. (Eds.), (1996). *Family group conferences*. Monsey: Willow Tree Press.

Imber-Black, E. (1988). *Families and larger systems: A family therapist's guide through the labyrinth*. New York: Guilford.

Kempe, C., Silverman, F., Steele, B., Droegemuller, W., & Silver, H. (1962). The battered baby syndrome. *Journal of the American Medical Association, 181*, 4–11.

Kempe, R.S., & Kempe, C. (1978). *Child abuse*. London: Fontana/Open Books.

Keys, T. (1996). Family decision making in Oregon. *Protecting Children, 12(3)*, 11–14.

Jeffreys, H., & Stevenson, M. (1997). *Statutory social work in a child protection agency: A guide for practice*. Whyalla: University of South Australia.

Lipchik, E. (1993). Both/and solutions. In S. Friedman (Ed.), *The new language of change: Constructive collaboration in psychotherapy*. New York: Guilford.

Little, M. (1995). Child protection or family support? Finding a balance: *Family Matters, 40(Autumn)*, 18–21.

Lusk, A. (1996). *The significance of denial in child abuse work: The professional construction of risk*. Unpublished master's dissertation, University of Wales, Cardiff.

MacKinnon, L. (1992). *Child abuse in context*. Unpublished Ph.D. thesis, University of Sydney, New South Wales.

MacKinnon, L. (1998). *Trust and betrayal in the treatment of child abuse*. New York: Guilford.

MacKinnon, L., & James, K. (1992a). Working with 'the welfare' in child-at risk cases, *Australian and New Zealand Journal of Family Therapy, 13(1)*, 1–15.

MacKinnon, L., & James, K. (1992b). Raising the stakes in child-at risk cases: Eliciting and maintaining parents' motivation. *Australian and New Zealand Journal of Family Therapy, 13(2)*, 59–71.

Magura, S., & Moses, B. (1984). Clients as evaluators in child protective services. *Child Welfare, 63(2),* 99–112.

Marsh, P. (1990). Changing practice in child care—the Children Act 1989. *Adoption and Fostering, 14(4),* 27–30.

Marsh, P. (1996). The development of FGCs—an overview. In K. Morris & J. Tunnard (Eds.), *Family group conferences: Messages from UK practice and research.* London: Family Rights Group.

Mason, J. (1989). In whose best interest? Some mother's experiences of child welfare interventions. *Australian Child and Family Welfare, 14(4),* 4–6.

Maxwell, G., & Morris, A. (1993). *Family victims of culture: Youth justice in New Zealand.* Victoria, New Zealand: University of Wellington.

Mayer, B. (1989). Mediation in child-protection cases. *Mediation Quarterly, 24,* 89–106.

McAllister, L.A. (1997). *Reforming the child welfare system through class action litigation: The Milwaukee case study.* Graduate paper, School of Social Work, University of Wisconsin, Madison.

McCallum, S. (1992). Participative case planning A model for empowering case planning in statutory child welfare. *Children Australia, 17(1),* 5–9.

McCallum, S. (1995). *Safe families: A model of child protection intervention based on parental voice and wisdom.* Unpublished Ph.D. thesis, Wilfrid Laurier University, Ontario, Canada.

McConkey, N. (1992). Working with adults to overcome the effects of sexual abuse: Integrating solution-focused therapy, systems thinking, and gender issues. *Journal of Strategic and Systemic Therapies, 11(3),* 4–19.

Merkel-Holguin, L. (1998, September). *Transferring the family group conferencing technology from New Zealand to the United States.* Paper presented at the Twelfth International Conference on Child Abuse and Neglect, Auckland, New Zealand.

Morris, K., & Tunnard, J. (Eds.), (1996). *Family group conferences: Messages from UK practice and research.* London: Family Rights Group.

Morrison, T. (1995). Partnership and collaboration: Rhetoric and reality. *Child Abuse and Neglect, 20(2),* 127–140.

O'Neil, D., & McCashen, W. (1991). Competency based family support: Brief therapy as a tool in goal setting and family valuing in child protection work. *Family Therapy Case Studies, 6(2),* 3–12.

Parton, N. (1985). *The politics of child abuse.* New York: St. Martin's Press.

Parton, N. (1996). Child protection, family support and social work: A critical reappraisal of the Department of Health research studies in child protection. *Child and Family Social Work, 1,* 3–11.

Parton, N., Thorpe, D., & Wattam, C. (1997). *Child protection: Risk and the moral order.* London: Macmillan.

Pelton, L.H. (1978). Child abuse and neglect: The myth of classlessness. *American Journal of Orthopsychiatry, 48(4),* 608–617.

Pelton, L.H. (1997). Child welfare policy and practice: The myth of family preservation. *American Journal of Orthopsychiatry, 67(4),* 545–553.

Perlman, H. (1972). The problem solving model in social casework. In R. Roberts & R. Nee (Eds.), *Theory of social casework*. Chicago: University of Chicago Press.

Pugh, G., & De Ath, E. (1985). *The needs of parents*. London: Macmillan.

Ralph, S. (1997). Working with Aboriginal families: Issues and guidelines for family and child counselors. *Family Matters, 46*, 46–50.

Rooney, R.H. (1998). Socialization strategies for involuntary clients. *Social Casework, March*, 131–140.

Rose, A survivor of our social services. (1991) *Rose's story*. Milwaukee: International Families Services Press.

Ryburn, M., & Atherton, C. (1996). Family group conferences: Partnership in practice. *Adoption and Fostering, 20(1)*, 16–23.

Sabotta, E., & Davies, R. (1992). Fatality after report to a child abuse registry in Washington State 1973–86. *Child Abuse and Neglect, 16*, 627–635.

Saleeby, D. (Ed.). (1992). *The strengths perspective in social work practice*. New York: Longman.

Scott, D., & O'Neil, D. (1996). *Beyond child rescue: Developing family-centered practice at St. Lukes*. Sydney: Allen and Unwin.

Schumacher, F. (1973). *Small is beautiful*. New York: Harper and Row.

Sharland, E., Jones, D., Aldgate, J., Seal, H., & Croucher, M. (1995). *Professional intervention in child sexual abuse*. London: HSMO.

Sigurdson, E., & Reid, G. (1996). *The Manitoba risk estimation© reference manual (version 4.8)*. Manitoba: Sigurdson, Reid and Associates Ltd.

Smart, R. (1994). Expertosis: Is it catching? *The Australian and New Zealand Journal of Family Therapy, 15*, 1–9.

Strathern, B. (1995). Risk assessment: Structured decision making. *Social Work Review*, June, 2–5.

The Center for Study of Social Policy. (1996). From investigation to assessment in Iowa. *Safekeeping, 1(Winter)*, 2–3.

Thoburn, J., Lewis, A., & Shemmings, D. (1995). *Paternalism or partnership? Family involvement in the child protection process*. London: HSMO.

Thomas, G. (1995). *Travels in the trench between child welfare theory and practice*. New York: Haworth.

Thompson, R.A. (1995). *Preventing child maltreatment through social support. A critical analysis*. Thousand Oaks, CA: Sage.

Thorpe, D. (1994). *Evaluating child protection Practice*. Birmingham: Open University Press.

Tomison, A. (1995). Protecting children the national picture, *National Child Protection Clearing House Newsletter, 3(2)*, 4–5.

Turnell, A., & Edwards, S. (1997). Aspiring to partnership: The signs of safety approach to child protection. *Child Abuse Review, 6*, 179–190.

Turnell, A., & Hopwood, L. (1994a). Solution-focused brief therapy: A first session outline. *Case Studies in Brief and Family Therapy, 8(2)*, 39–51.

Turnell, A., & Hopwood, L. (1994b). Solution-focused brief therapy: An outline for second and subsequent sessions. *Case Studies in Brief and Family Therapy, 8(2)*, 52–64.

U.S. Department of Health and Human Services, National Center on Child Abuse and Neglect, National Child Abuse and Neglect Data System. (1997). *Child maltreatment 1995: Reports from the states to the National Center on Child Abuse and Neglect*. Washington, DC: U.S. Government Printing Office.

Watzlawick, P., Weakland, J.H., & Fisch, R. (1974). *Change: Principles of problem formation and problem resolution*. New York: Norton.

Weakland, J.H., Fisch, R., Watzlawick, P., & Bodin, A. (1974). Brief therapy: Focused problem resolution. *Family Process, 13*, 141–168.

Weakland, J., & Jordan, L. (1990). Working briefly with reluctant clients: Child protection services as an example. *Family Therapy Case Studies, 5(2)*, 51–68.

Weick, A., Rapp, C., Sullivan, W., & Kishardt, W. (1989). A strengths perspective for social work practice. *Social Work, 34*, 350–354.

White, M. (1988). The externalising of the problem and the re-authoring of lives and relationships. *Dulwich Centre Newsletter*, Spring.

Winefield, H.R., & Barlow, J.A. (1995). Client and worker satisfaction in a child protection agency. *Child Abuse and Neglect, 19(8)*, 897–905.

Zellman, G.L., & Antler, S. (1990). Mandated reporters and CPS: A study in frustration. *Public Welfare, 48(1)*, 30–37.

Index

211